A COURSE ON C

A Course on C

Colin Charlton, Paul Leng and Janet Little

Department of Computer Science
University of Liverpool

McGRAW-HILL BOOK COMPANY

London · New York · St Louis · San Francisco · Auckland
Bogotá · Caracas · Hamburg · Lisbon · Madrid · Mexico · Milan
Montreal · New Delhi · Panama · Paris · San Juan · São Paulo
Singapore · Sydney · Tokyo · Toronto

Published by
McGRAW-HILL Book Company Europe
SHOPPENHANGERS ROAD · MAIDENHEAD · BERKSHIRE
SL6 2QL ENGLAND
TEL: 0628 23432; FAX: 0628 770224

British Library Cataloguing in Publication Data
Charlton, Colin
A Course on C
I. Title
005.13

ISBN 0–07–707433–5

Library of Congress Cataloging-in-Publication Data
Charlton, Colin.
A course on C / Colin Charlton, Paul Leng, and Janet Little.
p. cm.
Includes bibliographical references and index.
1. C (Computer program language) I. Leng, Paul. II. Little, Janet
III. Title.
QA76.73.C15C46 1992
005.13'3—dc20   92–31702
                                                             CIP

12345 PB 96543

Typeset by Charlton, Leng and Little and printed and bound in Great Britain by Page Bros, Norwich

For
Margaret, Zoe, Daniel, Caroline, Georgina, Ellen and George,
Gwynne, William, Mary and Thomas,
Tess, Bob, Ann, Tony, Mark and Maria

Contents

Preface

From modest beginnings, the C programming language has, over the past decade, become established as the closest to a common tongue to be found in the computing community. Its range of applications extends from the fields of scientific and commercial computing to low-level systems programming. Almost uniquely, its implementations span the range of computer power, from microcomputers to the most powerful multiprocessing machines.

The reasons for this success need not concern us here; they have something to do with the simplicity and efficiency with which C can be implemented, and much to do with the association between C and the UNIX operating system, with whose rise to prominence it has ridden in tandem. The result, however, has been that knowledge of C has become an essential part of the repertoire of almost every professional programmer.

Despite this, C remains an unpopular choice for a *first* programming language, to be used to learn the principles of computers and programming. Its style is too austere, and its roots too close to its low-level origins for it to appeal to beginners, who too readily encounter its pitfalls. It is likely to remain the professional's choice; the language that every serious programmer must learn *after* he or she has first mastered the concepts of a friendlier high-level language.

This book is intended for this kind of programmer. Assuming, as we do, that the reader begins with an understanding of computing concepts and of high-level language programming, we present a complete but relatively succinct description of ANSI-standard C. We avoid lengthy explanations of ideas with which we expect the reader to be familiar, but instead add detail and depth to the presentation by the inclusion of programming examples to illustrate both basic ideas and relatively complex applications, including the manipulation of list and tree structures. With the needs of the practical programmer in mind, also, we include a discussion of the use of C in mixed-language programming.

We hope thus to provide a book that will be of value to both professional programmers and to undergraduate and graduate students learning C as a 'second' language. It is based on an intensive one-week course which has been given on a number of occasions to groups of professional programmers; it is intended to serve as a text for similar courses, for university and other courses pursued over a longer period of time, or, alternatively, as a handbook for a programme of self-instruction. Our thanks are due to all those students on whom we have tested our ideas on programming in C, and also to Ken Chan, Jim Watt, and our other colleagues in the Liverpool University Department of Computer Science.

Chapter 1

A first C program

1.1 Introduction

One of the difficulties encountered in learning a new programming language is that there is usually quite a lot of detail to understand before even a simple program can be written. Rather than starting in this way, we begin by looking at a complete, very simple, C program. While the overall sense of the program is probably apparent to readers who are familiar with other high-level languages, an explanation of most of the details included will be deferred until the next chapter.

The intention behind the way in which this book is organized is that the reader should, where possible, follow the text by trying out program examples, as they are introduced, on the computer system that he or she is using. The practical details concerning the way in which this is done will, of course, be different for different systems. In introducing practical illustrations of programs in execution, we assume that you are making use of a system in which program text and other information is stored in named **files**, and that the system responds to **commands** issued by the user in response to **prompts** from the system. These basic characteristics are common to almost all systems. When we require to illustrate an example with the use of particular system commands or other system-dependent features, we will use the *italic* font to make clear that these details may be different on different systems. We expect that there will be no difficulty in your recognizing the equivalent features appropriate to the system you are using.

A simple C program

The example program of Figure 1.1 should, when executed, print one of three messages in each of three different cases.

```
/*  A simple greeting program  */

#include <stdio.h>

main(int argc,char *argv[])
{
  if (argc==2)
  {
    printf("Hello %s, hope you enjoy the course\n",
           argv[1]);
    exit(0);
  }
  else if (argc==1)
  {
    printf("Tell me your name & I'll say hello\n");
    exit(1);
  }
  else
  {
    printf("Too many parameters to the program\n");
    exit(1);
  }
}
```

Figure 1.1   A first simple program

Many of the elements of this program are apparent by analogy with other programming languages. These include:

- **Declarations** to introduce names of program variables, e.g.:
  ```
  int argc;
  ```

- **Statements** that will be executed by the program, e.g.:
  ```
  printf("Tell me your name & I'll say hello\n");
  ```

- **Comments** that are used to annotate the program. In C a comment is enclosed within the pairs of characters /* and */, thus:

```
/* this is a comment */
```

One other feature of the structure of a C program may need a little explanation at this point. In general, a C program contains declarations of one or more **functions** that define the algorithms involved in its execution. One of these functions is given the function name 'main' to indicate that this is the main procedure invoked when the program is executed. In Figure 1.1, this is the only function defined.

The body of a function consists of a sequence of statements (and, possibly, declarations) enclosed within a pair of 'curly' brackets: { and }. These brackets have a similar purpose in C to the keywords begin and end in Pascal and other languages. In this example, the body of the function main commences after the first { symbol and continues to the end of the program, defining a sequence of statements which will be performed when the function—i.e. in this case, the entire program—is executed. Notice also that there are other occurrences of curly brackets *within* the body of the function. In these cases, the brackets are being used to delimit blocks of statements, again in the same way as begin and end are used in other structured programming languages.

Program parameters

Like **procedures** and **subroutines** in other languages, a C function may be supplied with **parameters** (arguments), the purpose of which is to provide extra information for use in its execution. We will return to explain function arguments in more detail later. In order to understand the program illustrated in Figure 1.1, however, we need to explain briefly the special role of these arguments in the case where the function has the name main and is therefore invoked when a command to execute the program is given. In this case the parameters are **command-line arguments** that are supplied to the program when the command to execute it is given. The first argument (in this case, given the identifier argc) is given a value which defines the number of text words on the command line used to execute the program. The second argument, argv, defines an **array** to contain these words, allowing them to be individually inspected by the program.

Compiling and running the program

Let us suppose the program of Figure 1.1 is contained in a file with the filename *firstprog.c.* To **compile** this program, we give the command:

$ ccompile firstprog.c welcome

Here, we are using the symbol *$* to represent the prompt issued by the system. We assume the system will recognize the command *ccompile* and will, in this case, respond by compiling the C source program in the file *firstprog.c* to create an object-program file named *welcome*. Again it is necessary to note that these details are system-dependent, although it is likely that there will be a very close equivalent on the system you are using.

At the conclusion of the compilation, the file *welcome* will contain the compiled object program. To run this program, we assume the following command is used:

$ welcome `Colin`

In this case, there are two words ('*welcome*' and '`Colin`') on the command line, so the program is invoked with **argc** being given the value 2, resulting in the first of its three messages being printed:

```
$ welcome Colin
   Hello Colin, hope you enjoy the course
$
```

Within the program, the parameter **argv[1]** has been used to reference the command-line argument '`Colin`'. Had we invoked the program with no command-line argument, a different response would have been given:

```
$ welcome
   Tell me your name & I'll say hello
$
```

In this case **argc** has the value 1, so the program executes a different case.

Many programs, of course, do not make use of command-line arguments; more usually, as in other high-level languages, **data** is presented to the program via statements obeyed during its execution. We have introduced command-line arguments at this early stage, however, to emphasize the central role of the **function** in the construction of a C program. The simple program of Figure 1.1 takes the form of a single function, which is invoked by a **call** from the external software environment; i.e. in this case, from the operating system command environment.

1.2 Program inspection

Usually, when programming in a high-level language, it is quite unnecessary to be aware of the details of how the program is represented internally within the memory of the computer. Because C is designed to be used not only for high-level applications but also for systems programming, in which close control of machine-level operation is sometimes necessary, it is in some respects a lower-level language than, say, Pascal or FORTRAN. For this reason, some aspects of the machine-level implementation of C programs are made explicit in the definition of the language. Consequently, it is sometimes useful, and occasionally necessary, to examine a C program in execution by studying the changes of state it invokes in the underlying machine on which it is implemented.

Most C language programming environments provide some simple debugging tools to enable us to monitor a program in execution and examine details of the memory space it occupies. Their implementation is inevitably system-dependent; however, many of the features provided, such as facilities for inspecting memory and setting breakpoints, are common to most such tools. Because we will want, from time to time throughout this book, to illustrate through examples aspects of the way in which C programs are represented in memory, we will postulate a simple debugging system to enable us to do this. As with other aspects of our hypothetical programming environment, we expect that the reader will have no difficulty relating the commands we describe to the details of the real system that he or she is using.

We will suppose that the command:

```
$ cdebug <filename>
```

has the effect of compiling a C program contained in the named file, and loading the resulting object program under the control of the debugging system. Subsequent commands to this system enable us to monitor the state of the program during its execution. Commands to the debugging system, we will suppose, are entered in response to a question-mark (?) prompt.

Suppose, for example, we wish to study the execution of a program contained in a file called *shareout.c*. We first compile this under the control of the debugging system:

```
$ cdebug shareout.c
?
```

The ensuing question-mark prompt tells us that it has compiled without errors and that the debugging system is ready to accept a command.

The command:

> *? list*

gives us a line-numbered listing of the source program which we can use for reference (Figure 1.2).

```
 1: /* Program from file shareout.c
 2:  * Share out the spoils between
 3:  * the number in the gang
 4:  */
 5:
 6: #include <stdio.h>
 7:
 8:  main()
 9:  {
10:     int num_in_gang;
11:     float loot,my_share;
12:
13:     printf("Enter 'amount' and 'gang size'\n");
14:     scanf("%f%d",&loot,&num_in_gang);
15:
16:     my_share = loot/num_in_gang;
17:     printf("my share comes to %f\n",my_share);
18:  }
```

Figure 1.2   A program being debugged

Before we go on to execute the object program, we set a **breakpoint** at line 16; this has the effect of halting the program at the point in execution which corresponds to the start of this line:

> *? setbreakpoint 16*

Now when we go on to run the program, it executes normally up to this point:

```
? run
Enter 'amount' and 'gang size'
33.3    3
breakpoint at line 16
?
```

The message:

Enter 'amount' and 'gang size'

was displayed as part of the normal execution of the program, as a result of the statement on line 13, and the numbers on the following line were typed as input required at line 14. On reaching line 16, the program has halted its execution, and the debugging system has printed a message to show that a breakpoint has been reached. We may now, if we wish, inspect the values of the program variables.

```
? show loot
33.3
? show num_in_gang
3
? show my_share
11.099999
?
```

Finally, we may allow the program to proceed to completion:

```
? continue

my share comes to 11.099999
program terminated
? quit
$
```

The *quit* command returns the system to the normal command-mode context, indicated by the succeeding dollar prompt.

Debugging this very simple program has not, of course, told us anything that is not clear from the normal output of the program. We have introduced the bare outlines of this simple hypothetical debugging system at this point, however, so that we can use it later to illustrate aspects of the machine-level organization of C programs that may not otherwise be apparent. Meanwhile, the reader may find it helpful to investigate the debugging facilities which are available on the system that he or she is using, and to try them out on the simple program examples we have introduced.

1.3   Exercises

1. Find out how to compile and execute the program *firstprog.c* of Figure 1.1, on the system you are using.

2. When you have executed the program successfully, investigate the effects of introducing some minor grammatical errors to the program; for example, change one of the instances of `argc` to `argd`. When you recompile the program, a compile-time error should ensue, with a corresponding error message produced. Try a few other errors, such as removing one of the curly brackets, to find out what error messages are produced in each case.

3. For the program *shareout.c* of Figure 1.2, investigate the effect of giving the value 0 for `num_in_gang` when the program is executed.

4. Find out what program debugging tools are available on the system you are using. If possible, find out how to set a breakpoint; inspect the value of a program variable; continue from a breakpoint; and unset a breakpoint. Use the programs of Figures 1.1 and 1.2 to familiarize yourself with the facilities offered.

Chapter 2

Basic elements of C

2.1 Functions and declarations

In outline, a C program is expressed as a sequence of **declarations**. These must include the declaration of one 'main' program **function** that is invoked when the program is executed. Other functions may be defined that are invoked, directly or indirectly, by **calls** from the main program function.

The program of Figure 2.1 contains declarations of three functions: the main program function, `main()`, and two others, `min()` and `max()`. Notice the convention we now use in referring to a function; writing a pair of brackets following the function name indicates that `max()`, for example, is a function rather than some other program element. Within the program, the brackets contain a specification of the **parameters** of the function. Even when there are no such parameters, however, as in the case of the function `main()` in this example, the brackets are still included to indicate that this is the name of a function.

In this example, the main program function determines and displays the largest and smallest of three numbers presented as data. It does so by making use of the function `min()`, which **returns** as its result the value of the smaller of two numbers, and `max()`, which returns the value of the larger of two numbers. Notice the broad similarities in the structure of the three functions declared: in each case, the **body** of the function, enclosed within curly brackets { and }, defines the sequence of declarations and statements performed in carrying out the function. Essentially, the main program function is no different from other functions that may be declared within the program, which is why the concept of a function is more fundamental to the C language than is, for example, the **subroutine** in FORTRAN.

9

```
/* Program to find the largest and smallest of
 * three integers.
 */

#include <stdio.h>

int little,large;

/*----------------------------------------------------------*/

int min(int first, int second)
{
    if (first<second) return first;
    else return second;
}

/*----------------------------------------------------------*/

int max(int first, int second)
{
    if (first>second) return first;
    else return second;
}

/*----------------------------------------------------------*/

main()
{
    int num1,num2,num3;

    printf("Type three integers separated by spaces\n");
    scanf("%d%d%d",&num1,&num2,&num3);

    little=min(num1,num2);
    large=max(num1,num2);
    little=min(little,num3);
    large=max(large,num3);

    printf("The littlest=%d the largest=%d\n",little,large);
}
```

Figure 2.1   A program including three functions

Before we go on to look in detail at the way functions are defined and used, however, we need to understand the other kinds of declaration that can occur in a C program. In the program of Figure 2.1, there are a number of declarations of program **variables**.

Variables

In Figure 2.1, the line

```
int little,large;
```

is a declaration of two variables. The declaration associates with each variable three properties: a **name**, a **data type**, and a **storage class**. In the example, the two variables declared are given the names `little` and `large`. In general, a name can be any sequence of alphabetic and numeric characters, possibly also including the underscore character, provided that the sequence does not start with a digit. Examples include the following:

```
first_time   temp       class_of_90
A_register   max_size   START
ODDaddress   counter    DONT_PANIC
```

Note that names are **case-dependent**; that is, `fred` and `FRED` are two different names. In principle, there is no limit on the length of a name, although particular C language implementations may impose a limit that (in ANSI C) must be no less than 31 characters. The only other restriction on the choice of names is that a number of identifiers are reserved for use as **keywords** in the C language, and cannot therefore be used as names of variables. These keywords are itemized in Figure 2.2.

```
auto      break     case    char     const   continue
default   do        double  else     entry   enum
extern    float     for     goto     if      int
long      register  return  short    sizeof  static
signed    struct    switch  typedef  union   unsigned
void      volatile  while
```

Figure 2.2   C keywords

Data types

The **data type** of a program variable defines the characteristics of the
data object to which it refers. More specifically, it determines the size of
the storage element which will be used to contain the value of the variable,
and also how this value will be interpreted when the program is executed. In
our example, `little` and `large` are of type int (integer), so these variables
will be treated as having values which are signed integers. The precise way
in which values of a particular type are represented within the memory is
a system-dependent feature, as is also the size of the storage element used.
This means that the permissible range of values of a variable of type `int`,
for example, will vary between different C implementations.

Figure 2.3 lists the **inbuilt** data types of the C language, with examples
of possible implementation sizes and consequent ranges of values. As well
as these, C enables **user-defined** types to be introduced, allowing more
complex data objects such as arrays to be declared; we will return to this
in Chapter 3.

type	possible size	values
char	8 bits	0 to 255
short short int	16 bits	-32768 to 32767
int	32 bits	-2147483648 to 2147483647
long long int	32 bits	-2147483648 to 2147483647
float	32 bits	real numbers to about 6 sig. figs.
double	64 bits	real numbers to about 15 sig. figs.
long double	128 bits	real numbers to about 33 sig. figs.

Figure 2.3   Inbuilt data types

Note that, although three different integer types can be used (`int, short
int` and `long int`), these need not represent different sizes; in the illustra-
tion in Figure 2.3, `int` and `long int` both refer to values of size 32 bits.
The only restrictions on possible implementations are that `short int` and
`int` must be at least 16 bits, and `long int` at least 32 bits, in length. Similarly, `float`, `double` and `long double` may or may not represent different
sizes of variable.

The types `int` (including `short` and `long`) and `char` may be prefixed
with the qualifier `signed` or `unsigned`. Thus, for example, a variable of
type `unsigned int` of size 32 bits would have possible values in the range

0 to 4294967296, and a `signed char` of size 8 bits would have values in the range −128 to +127. The implementation of `char` itself may be either `unsigned` (as in Figure 2.3) or `signed`.

The program of Figure 2.4 prints out as a table the ranges of values of the various inbuilt data types, including signed and unsigned alternatives. These ranges are defined as a set of C language constants, `INT_MIN`, `LONG_MAX`, etc., which have implementation-dependent values. Running this program on the system you are using will tell you the relevant values for your ANSI C implementation.

Storage classes

The **storage class** of a variable defines its **scope** (the part of the program within which it can be used) and its **lifetime** (the duration of its existence). The storage class may be defined explicitly or (as in the examples we have seen so far) implied by the position of the declaration within the program. There are four possible storage classes, of which the two most important are `extern` and `auto`.

Variables of the storage class `extern` (**external**) are **global**: their scope is the entire program, and their lifetime is the duration of the program's execution. A variable has storage class `extern` if its declaration takes place *outside* any function in the program. In Figure 2.1, `little` and `large` are of this storage class because their declaration is outside the function declarations. They are thus global variables that may be used (referred to) within any of the functions of the program. Note, however, that a variable must be declared *before* it is used, so it is usual for global declarations to occur at the start of the program.

Variables declared *within* the body of a function are of `auto` (**automatic**) storage class, which implies that they are **local** to the function. In Figure 2.1, `num1,num2` and `num3` are of this storage class: they are local to the function `main()`, and cannot be referred to directly within the other functions defined. The scope of a local variable is the body of the function within which it is declared, and its lifetime is the duration of the invocation (call) of that function; that is, its value is lost when the function terminates. The **formal parameters** of a function, whose declaration is made within the brackets following the function name, have similar characteristics to local variables declared within the function body. In Figure 2.1, `first` and `second` are formal parameters which are local to the function `min()`. The function `max()` has formal parameters with the same names, but the rules of **scope** imply that these are treated as two quite distinct pairs of variables.

The two other storage classes are introduced briefly here:

```
/* To print out a table of the ranges of the
 * primitive data types.
 */

#include <stdio.h>
#include <limits.h>
#include <float.h>

main()
{
   printf("%-20s%3d bits    %d to %d\n","char",
          sizeof(char)*8,CHAR_MIN,CHAR_MAX);
   printf("%-20s%3d bits    %d to %d\n","signed char",
          sizeof(signed char)*8,SCHAR_MIN,SCHAR_MAX);
   printf("%-20s%3d bits    %u to %u\n","unsigned char",
          sizeof(unsigned char)*8,0,UCHAR_MAX);
   printf("%-20s%3d bits    %d to %d\n","short",
          sizeof(short)*8,SHRT_MIN,SHRT_MAX);
   printf("%-20s%3d bits    %u to %u\n","unsigned short",
          sizeof(unsigned short)*8,0,USHRT_MAX);
   printf("%-20s%3d bits    %d to %d\n","int",
          sizeof(int)*8,INT_MIN,INT_MAX);
   printf("%-20s%3d bits    %u to %u\n","unsigned",
          sizeof(unsigned)*8,0,UINT_MAX);
   printf("%-20s%3d bits    %ld to %ld\n","long",
          sizeof(long)*8,LONG_MIN,LONG_MAX);
   printf("%-20s%3d bits    %lu to %lu\n","unsigned long",
          sizeof(unsigned long)*8,0,ULONG_MAX);
   printf("%-20s%3d bits    %g to %g "
          "with %3d digits of precision\n","float",
          sizeof(float)*8,FLT_MIN,FLT_MAX,FLT_DIG);
   printf("%-20s%3d bits    %g to %g "
          "with %3d digits of precision\n","double",
          sizeof(double)*8,DBL_MIN,DBL_MAX,DBL_DIG);
   printf("%-20s%3d bits    %Lg to %Lg "
          "with %3d digits of precision\n","long double",
          sizeof(long double)*8,LDBL_MIN,LDBL_MAX,LDBL_DIG);
}
```

Figure 2.4   Displaying ranges of data types

- **static** storage class is used for a variable whose value will be pre-served between successive calls of a function.

- **register** storage class is used when we wish to optimize a program by explicitly allocating particular variables for storage in registers rather than in main memory.

These two classes will be described in more detail later.

Constant denotations

Within the body of a function, variables may be assigned values and sub-sequently used, for example, as terms in expressions. In Figure 2.1, initial values for the variables **num1**, **num2** and **num3** were obtained by reading data, but we can also, of course, give a value to a variable by direct assignment within the program; thus, for example:

num = 17;

In this example, and similar cases, we require to express a value in the form of a **constant denotation**. In this case, the denotation used is the integer 17, but we may also need to express values of any of the inbuilt types of C.

Integer constants

A constant of type **int** may be expressed in decimal, octal or hexadecimal form:

- **Decimal representation**: a sequence of digits, the first of which must *not* be 0 (zero).
  Example: **43721**

- **Octal representation**: a sequence of octal digits (range 0-7) *starting with* 0 (zero).
  Example: **027**

- **Hexadecimal representation**: a sequence of hexadecimal charac-ters (0-9, A, B, C, D, E, F or a, b, c, d, e, f) prefixed by **0X** or **0x**.
  Example: **0xffff**

The suffixes **l** or **L**, and **u** or **U**, can be added to any form of integer de-notation to specify **long** and **unsigned** representations respectively, when required. Thus:

51	is a long integer
23u	is an unsigned integer
0111117777L	is a long integer (in octal form)
0X71FFFFUL	is an unsigned, long integer (in hexadecimal form)

If no suffix L is present, a constant is still represented as a long integer if it is too large to be stored as of type int.

Real number constants

Real numbers (type float and double) can be represented in either of two forms:

- **Fixed point**: a sequence of decimal digits containing a decimal point.

- **Floating point**: an integer or fixed point number, followed by an **exponent** written as E (or e) followed by a signed integer.

Examples: 1.5
                    342.768345
                    72.1245E27
                    1e-123

The value of the exponent expresses a multiplication by a power of 10. Real number denotations are assumed to be of type double unless qualified by a suffix F or f (for float) or L or l (for long double).

Characters

Printable character constants are normally represented by enclosing the character symbol in single quotes, thus: 'A'. The character is represented internally using a numeric character coding, so that, if the usual ASCII code is used, 'A' will be stored as the number 65. Non-printable characters are represented using an **escape sequence**, the first character of which is **backslash** (\). The same convention is used to represent the characters \ and ' which would otherwise cause confusion. The complete set of escape sequences is defined in Figure 2.5.

In addition, an arbitrary character value can be written as an escape sequence using an octal representation, or a hexadecimal representation prefixed by the symbol x. Some examples of character constants:

'y'   ';'   '\n'   '\027'   '\"'   '\x3A'

\a	alert (bell)	\\	backslash
\b	backspace	\?	question mark
\f	form feed	\'	quote
\n	newline	\"	double quote
\r	carriage return	\0	null
\t	horizontal tab		
\v	vertical tab		

Figure 2.5   Escape sequences

Strings

A string is a sequence of characters enclosed in double quotes. It will be stored internally as the corresponding sequence of character values terminated by the **null character**. Included in the sequence may be any character expressed as an escape sequence. The null string (written as a pair of quotes with no character symbols enclosed) represents the null character only. The representation \n is used to represent a **newline** character in a string, so that breaking a string representation across two or more lines will not affect its value. Some examples:

```
       "Hello World"
     "\nring the bell \07"
            ""
   "\t column1 \t column2"
```

Symbolic constants

The program of Figure 2.4 used a number of predefined **symbolic constants** (CHAR_MIN, SHRT_MAX, LDBL_DIG, etc.) that represent particular implementation-dependent values. It is sometimes useful also to define our own symbolic constants, to allow numeric or character values to be given equivalent symbolic names in the program we are writing. We can do this using a **directive**, #define, which must be written starting at the first character-position in a line of the program. For example:

```
#define TEN 10
```

defines a symbolic constant, TEN, which is identically equal to the numeric constant 10. Note that TEN does not correspond to a program variable or constant value for which a memory location is allocated; it is a symbol which is equivalent to the number 10. Whenever we use the symbolic name

TEN, subsequently in the program, its effect will be the same as if we had written the numeric denotation **10**.

The structure of a function

Now let us look at the general form taken by a function declaration. We can express this (using a well-known notational convention) as follows:

> < *result type* > < *function name* > (< *parameter list* >)
> < *function body* >

Applying this to one of the functions declared in Figure 2.1:

```
< result type >
    |    < function name >
    |        |    < parameter list >
    ↓        ↓    ┌───────┴───────┐
int min(int first, int second)
{
    if (first<second) return first;    ┐
    else return second;                ├ < function body >
}                                      ┘
```

The **function name** defines an identifier that will be used to refer to the function when it is called to invoke its action. The **function body** is, as we have already seen, enclosed within a pair of curly brackets. It comprises a sequence of statements (and, possibly, declarations) that will be performed when the function is invoked.

The function body may include one or more **return statements** that define a result value to be produced by the execution of the function. In the example we are using, the result returned will be, in different cases, either the value of the parameter **first** or the parameter **second**. The **result type** specified in the function declaration defines the type that this returned value must have. Not every function is required to return a value: we can declare a function of this kind (the equivalent of a simple procedure or subroutine in other languages) by specifying the result type **void**. However, if we omit (as we may) the result type specification altogether, it will be taken *by default* to be of type **int**.

A function is invoked by a statement elsewhere in the program which calls it. For example, in the program of Figure 2.1, the statement:

```
/* Example of the use of some simple functions. */

#include <stdio.h>

/*-----------------------------------------------------------*/

float add(float x, float y)
{ return x+y; }

/*-----------------------------------------------------------*/

float sub(float x, float y)
{ if (x>y) return x-y; else return y-x; }

/*-----------------------------------------------------------*/

float average(float x, float y)
{ return (x+y)/2; }

/*-----------------------------------------------------------*/

void output_stats(float s, float d, float m)
{ printf("Sum = %f Difference = %f Mean = %f\n",s,d,m); }

/*-----------------------------------------------------------*/

main()
{
   float x,y,sum,diff,mean;

   /* input data */
   printf("input reals x and y\n");
   scanf("%f%f",&x,&y);

   /* compute statistics */
   sum = add(x,y);
   diff = sub(x,y);
   mean = average(x,y);

   /* output results */
   output_stats(sum,diff,mean);
}
```

Figure 2.6   A program using functions

```
little = min(num1,num2);
```

includes a call of the function `min()`, for which the values of the variables `num1` and `num2` are supplied as arguments, or **actual parameters**. In the function declaration, the types required for the function arguments are specified in the **parameter list**, which also declares names for the **formal parameters** that will be used within the function body to refer to the arguments. If the function has no parameters, then we may specify this by writing **void** within the brackets that normally define the parameter list. The parameter specification **void** can in fact be omitted entirely, and by convention this is usually done in the case of a `main()` function without parameters.

Figure 2.6 shows another example of a program that declares and uses a number of simple functions. We will need to return to describe the mechanisms involved in passing parameters and returning results in more detail, later in the book. We have introduced the general form of a function at this stage, however, because of the central role of functions in the C language. The simplest programs, as we have seen, comprise a single main function declaration; having discussed the structure of this, we go on to describe in more detail some of the kinds of **statement** which may be included in the function body.

2.2   Statements and expressions

As in other conventional, **imperative** programming languages such as FORTRAN or Pascal, program execution steps in C take the form of **statements**. Each statement defines an action in the algorithmic sequence and, in C, is terminated by a semicolon.

The basic statement type is the **assignment statement**, which gives a value to, or changes the value of, a previously declared variable. It takes the general form:

$$< variable > = < expression >;$$

The expression is evaluated to produce a result that is assigned to the variable on the left-hand side of the **assignment operator**, '='. The type declared for this variable determines the type of the result assigned; if evaluation of the expression does not produce a result of the required type, then a **type conversion** takes place on the value to allow the assignment to take place.

The expression itself is made up of terms that may include constant denotations, variables and function calls, which are combined and acted upon by **operators**.

Arithmetic expressions

In an arithmetic expression, the operators used are:

- **monadic** (unary) operators :
  - `+` unary plus
  - `-` negate
  - `++` increment
  - `--` decrement

- **diadic** operators:
  - `+` addition
  - `-` subtraction
  - `*` multiplication
  - `/` division
  - `%` modulo (remainder)

Most of these will be familiar from their use in other languages, and need no further explanation here. Addition, subtraction and multiplication apply in the same way to integer and real values. The division operator, '/', however, has a different effect in the two cases. If either of its operands is of one of the real-value types, **float**, **double** or **long double**, it will perform a real division to produce a result of the appropriate real-value type. If both operands are of type **int** (or **char**), an integer division is performed, producing an integer result which is **truncated**. The modulus operator, '%', also performs an integer division, but in this case the result produced is the remainder arising from the division. This operator cannot be applied to real-value operands.

The monadic operators `++` and `--` are unusual in that they can be used in either **prefix** or **postfix** forms. Their effect is to either increment or decrement the value of the variable to which they are applied. Depending on whether the prefix or postfix form is used, the value of the variable will be altered either before or after it is used in the expression. Thus the sequence:

```
x = 12; y = ++x;
```

will result in the integer variables **x** and **y** both having the value 13. This is because the prefix form of the `++` operator causes **x** to be incremented *before* its value is assigned to **y**. Conversely:

```
x = 12; y = x++;
```

would assign the value 12 to **y**, and subsequently increment **x** to give it the new value 13.

The increment and decrement operators are 'active' in the sense that they not only produce a value but also bring about a change in the value of their operand. For this reason, the operand must be (in the simplest case) a variable rather than, say, a constant. For all the simple types we have discussed so far, the value of the variable will be incremented or decremented by 1. For the same reason, we can use these operators to write increment and decrement statements without an assignment operator; the statement:

`x--;`

is equivalent to the assignment:

`x = x-1;`

In these cases the use of prefix or postfix form is immaterial. The use of increment and decrement operators in this way is often encouraged because it is likely that the compiler will be able to translate them into particularly concise and efficient object-code forms.

Operator precedence

Expressions containing more than one arithmetic operator are evaluated from left to right, subject to the rules of operator precedence. As in most other high-level languages, these rules prescribe that operators of a high priority are applied before those of a low priority. The order of priority, or precedence, of the operators described so far is:

highest	(monadic):	+	-	++	--
		*	/	%	
lowest	(diadic):	+	-		

Precedence can be overridden by the use of brackets in the usual way, thus:

`x = y*(a+3);`

will cause 3 to be added to a *before* multiplying the result by **y**. Without the use of brackets, the multiplication would take place before the addition because of its higher priority.

Type conversion and casts

As we have said, the result of the expression will, if necessary, be converted to conform to the type declared for the variable to which it is to be assigned. Type conversion may also take place within the expression if, for example, the operands of a particular operator are of different types.

A number of type conversions are **automatic**; they take place when not all the terms in the expression are of the same type. In general, the effect of these conversions is to change values of a 'lower' type into a 'higher' type within which they can be represented without loss of information. For example, if a value of type **int** is added to a **float** value, then it is converted to the corresponding **float**-type form before the addition takes place. In general, in mixed-mode expressions, values of type **char** and **short** are extended to be represented as type **int**; then, further conversions take place as required in the following sequence:

```
int ⇒
     unsigned int ⇒
                 long ⇒
                     unsigned long ⇒
                                 float ⇒
                                     double ⇒
                                         long double
```

The effect, in general, is to convert terms in a mixed-mode expression so that they are all represented in the more extended form, to allow arithmetic to take place without loss of precision. When the final assignment of the resulting value takes place, however, the type required is always that of the destination variable, so in this case the conversion may involve either an extension (e.g. **int** to **float**) or a truncation. Real-number types are truncated to integer form by removing the fractional part; a conversion of **double** to **float** may involve a loss of precision; and **long int** is converted to **int** by truncating from the high-order end of the representation. In all these, and other similar conversions, it is necessary for the programmer to take care to ensure that the type of the destination variable is sufficient to accommodate the value assigned without errors arising.

Finally, there are some cases where it is necessary for the programmer to force an explicit type conversion upon the result of an expression. This is achieved by a **cast**, which takes the form:

$$(< type >) < expression >$$

For example:

```
r = a+b/(int)(x+0.5);
```

This has the effect of **coercing** the result of the expression (x+0.5) to be of type **int** before the division into b takes place, so that (if b is of type **int**) an integer division will take place. Without the cast, normal type conversion rules would force the expression to be extended to a real-number type.

Note that the cast (`int`) (in this case) behaves like a monadic operator, with similar precedence; thus we must enclose the expression (`x+0.5`) in brackets to ensure that the cast applies to the whole expression rather than just the term `x`.

Multiple assignment

An assignment statement is, in fact, a special case of an **expression** which includes an assignment operator, '`=`'. This operator behaves in some ways differently from, for example, '`*`'; in particular, assignment associates from right to left rather than left to right (so that the right-hand side of the assignment operation is evaluated before the assignment takes place). However, like other expressions, an assignment expression produces a value, which is the same as the value assigned to the variable on the left of the assignment operator. Thus, if `a` is of type `int`:

$$a = 5$$

is an expression whose value is the integer 5.

The implication of this is that we can use such an expression as a term in a more complex expression; in particular, we can perform multiple assignments, such as:

$$b = a = 5$$

Because of the right-to-left association of the assignment operator, the assignment:

$$a = 5$$

will take place first; then the result of this expression (i.e. 5) will in turn be assigned to `b`.

Initialization of variables

It is, of course, good programming practice to ensure that each variable declared is explicitly assigned a value before it is used in any other way. In fact, **global** (external) variables are implicitly initialized automatically to the zero value, although this is *not* the case for local variables, whose initial value is undefined.

A variable can be given an explicit initial value by combining its declaration with an assignment; thus:

```
int count = 1;
char nl = '\n';
```

In a global declaration, the terms in the expression assigned must be constant values. When declaring local variables, however, values of previously assigned variables may be included in the expression. When we make a declaration in this way, we may also sometimes wish to specify that the value referred to by the identifier will not change, i.e. that it is a **constant**. We can do this with a declaration of the form (for example):

```
const float pi = 3.14159;
```

Boolean expressions

Unlike some other languages, C does not have an explicit type **boolean** to represent logical values (TRUE and FALSE). Instead these values are represented as integers, with the convention that 0 represents FALSE, and *any* non-zero integer value is interpreted as TRUE. A set of relational and logical operators that use this convention are provided. Thus, for example, the relation:

$$x > 5.2$$

is a boolean expression, the result of which will be the integer value 1 (if x is greater than 5.2), or 0 otherwise.

The full set of **relational operators** is:

```
==    equals
!=    not equals
>     greater than
>=    greater than or equals
<     less than
<=    less than or equals
```

Logical values, such as in particular the results of relational expressions, can be further combined in expressions using the **logical operators**:

```
&&    and
||    or
!     not
```

For example:

```
a>b && t==0
```

is true (expression evaluates to 1) if both a>b and t==0, and will otherwise evaluate to 0. Note that it is not necessary in this example to enclose the relations a>b and t==0 in brackets, as the relational operators have a higher precedence than the logical operators (although lower than arithmetic operators).

Bitwise operations

It is also possible in C to perform logical operations on bit patterns representing integer (or character) type operands. The operators & (AND), | (OR), ^ (exclusive-OR) and ~ (NOT) are represented thus to distinguish them from the corresponding boolean operators. Bitwise logical operations are applied bit-by-bit to corresponding bits of their operands. AND (&) is usually used to mask off particular bits; for example, the statement:

```
        /* extract the low order byte */

        w = w & 0xff;
```

```
    w          10100000110011111010111011011011
    0xff       00000000000000000000000011111111   &
              ------------------------------------
  w & 0xff     00000000000000000000000011011011
              ------------------------------------
```

OR(|) is usually used to include particular bits:

```
        /* set sign bit to 1 */

        x = x | 0x80000000;
```

```
    x              00100100110011001010111011011010
    0x80000000     10000000000000000000000000000000   |
                  ------------------------------------
  x | 0x80000000   10100100110011001010111011011010
                  ------------------------------------
```

Exclusive OR(^) is used to test if bits are the same or different. (0 results if bits are the same, 1 if different):

```
y = y ^ 0x7a34ffff;
```

```
y            00000000000000001010101010101010
0x7a34ffff   01111010001101001111111111111111   ^
             ----------------------------------
y ^ 0x7a34ffff 01111010001101000101010101010101
             ----------------------------------
```

The bitwise NOT, or **ones complement** operator (˜), is monadic; its effect is to invert each bit of its operand:

```
z = ˜z;
```

```
z            00001111100111110000101010101111   ˜
             ----------------------------------
˜z           11110000011000001111010101010000
             ----------------------------------
```

Bit patterns can also be shifted left to right, using the shift operators `<<` and `>>`. The left-shift operator performs a logical shift, introducing zeros at the low-order end of the representation:

```
x = x<<2;
```

```
x            00000000000000000000000001101101   <<
             ----------------------------------
x << 2       00000000000000000000000110110100
             ----------------------------------
```

A right shift of an **unsigned** quantity is also a logical shift, introducing eros at the high-order end. Right shifts of **signed** quantities are, however, machine-dependent; they may be implemented either as logical shifts or as arithmetic shifts in which the sign bit is propagated.

Precedence of arithmetic, logical and bitwise operators

Because both logical operations and bitwise operations apply, essentially, to integer-type operands, and because the type conversion rules of C permit most forms of mixed-mode expression, we may often find expressions which include mixtures of arithmetic, logical and bitwise operators. In these cases, the priority of evaluation is determined by the following precedence table:

highest	(monadic):	+	–	++	--	! ~
		*	/	%		
	(diadic):	+	–			
		<<	>>			
		<	<=	>	>=	
		==	!=			
		&				
		^				
		|				
		&&				
		||				
lowest		=				

Note the low priority of '=' means that the right-hand side of an assignment is always evaluated before assignment takes place.

2.3   Input and output functions

Input and output operations in C are performed using **library functions**. While alternatives may be available in some systems, all complete ANSI C implementations should include a **standard library** of functions to perform these and other common operations in a defined way. To make use of the input and output functions from this library, we must include in the program the directive:

```
#include <stdio.h>
```

This is normally the first line of the program file, and must be written (like #define) starting at the first character-position in the line. We will say more about libraries and #include in Chapter 5; for the moment, it is sufficient to know that this line enables the program to make use of a set of input and output functions defined in the standard library.

getchar and putchar

The simplest input and output functions are those which perform single character transput. The function getchar() reads a single character as input, delivering its value; thus:

```
next = getchar();
```

results in a single character being assigned to the variable **next**. The source of the input is system-dependent, and defined by the standard library, but we may assume that it is from the user's keyboard.

Similarly, the function **putchar()** prints or displays a character on the standard output device, which is usually the user's terminal screen. The parameter of this function defines the character to be printed:

```
putchar(some_char_variable);
putchar('A');
```

Formatted output

More general forms of data output are provided by the formatted output function **printf()**. Calls of this function take the general form:

$$\text{printf}(< format\ string >,\ < argument\ list >);$$

This will cause a sequence of arguments from the $< argument\ list >$ to be printed or displayed on the standard output device (usually the terminal screen) in a format determined by the $< format\ string >$. An instance from the program of Figure 2.1 illustrates the main points:

```
printf("The littlest=%d the largest=%d\n",little,large);
```

Here, the arguments are the variables **little** and **large** whose values are displayed. In general, arguments of **printf()** may be variables, constant values, or expressions which are evaluated for output.

The $< format\ string >$ defines the way in which these values are displayed. It contains both literal characters (including escape sequences such as \n) which are printed directly, and **conversion specifications** which are used to define the format in which values in the $< argument\ list >$ are expressed. The conversion specifications are prefixed with the character %, and are matched in turn with arguments in the $< argument\ list >$. In this example, the format %d, specifying output as a signed decimal integer, is used twice, referring respectively to the arguments **little** and **large**. Thus if **little** and **large** have the values 3 and 10 respectively, the output produced is:

```
The littlest=3 the largest=10
```

followed by a new line. We can also omit the $< argument\ list >$ entirely, in which case the only output is the characters from the $< format\ string >$. If the format string is too long to be contained on one line, it can be divided

into two or more strings, each separately enclosed in quotes; the program
of Figure 2.4 included some examples of this.

The set of conversion specification codes used by `printf()` is listed in
Figure 2.7. With the exception of `%p`, which will be explained when we come
to discuss **pointers** in C, these are straightforward specifications for the
output of integer, real and character values in various forms. It is of course
necessary for the programmer to ensure that these are matched sensibly to
the arguments listed, in the correct order.

`%d`	signed decimal integer
`%i`	signed decimal integer
`%o`	unsigned octal integer
`%u`	unsigned decimal integer
`%x`	unsigned hexadecimal integer (using a,b,c,d,e,f)
`%X`	unsigned hexadecimal integer (using A,B,C,D,E,F)
`%f`	decimal point notation
`%e(%E)`	floating point with exponent indicated by e(E)
`%g(%G)`	uses the shorter of `%f` or `%e(%E)`
`%c`	character
`%s`	string
`%p`	a pointer to void
`%%`	print %

Figure 2.7   Conversion specification codes for `printf()`

One other pseudo-conversion specification is used to enable the number
of characters output in a `printf()` call to be recorded. Inclusion of the
specification `%n` in the < *format string* > results in a value equal to the
number of characters printed up to this point being assigned to the corresponding argument in the < *argument list* >. In this case, the argument
must refer to a variable of integer type, which we write as `&i` (where i is
the variable name); the significance of the `&` symbol will become clear in
the next chapter. No output is produced by the `%n` specification itself.

The normal printable conversion specification codes may be prefixed by
various qualifiers to give finer control over the format of the output. The
following examples illustrate this:

`%10s`	string printed in a (minimum of) 10-character field (padded with leading spaces if necessary)
`%8.2f`	real number printed in a 8-character field, with 2 decimal places

%-6d	integer left-justified in a 6-character field
%06d	printed with leading zeros
%+5d	sign of number always printed
%10.6s	6 characters (at most) from argument printed in a 10-character field
% 4d	positive number prefixed by space

Note that values printed are normally right-justified (unless the '−' qualifier is used) and padded with spaces (unless the qualifier '0' is used with a numeric format).

Additionally, the integer codes d,i,o,u,x, and X may be immediately prefixed by one of the letters l or L, to indicate long integer, or h to indicate short integer.

Some examples of the use of printf() are given below. For illustration, we have used literal values as arguments; more usually, of course, these would be variables or expressions. A further example is included as Figure 2.8, which illustrates the use of printf() to output values in different number formats.

```
printf("What's your name? %6s where do you live? %s\n",
       "MARY JANE","down the lane");
What's your name? MARY JANE where do you live? down the lane
```

(The specification %6s is the *minimum* field width, so all characters of MARY JANE are printed.)

```
printf("What's your name? %4.6s where do you live? %s\n",
       "MARY JANE","down the lane");
What's your name? MARY J where do you live? down the lane
```

(%4.6s implies a minimum of 4 and a maximum of 6 characters.)

```
printf("What's your number? %+04d\n",7);
What's your number? +007
```

```
printf("To the left %-4d and to the right %4d\n",1,2);
To the left 1    and to the right    2
```

```
printf("beep \07beep\07 \tand beep  again%c\n",7);
beep beep         and beep again
```

```
/* This program demonstrates the ability of printf() to
 * output in different formats */

#include <stdio.h>

/*--------------------------------------------------------------*/

void output_table(int limit)
{
   int i;

   printf("\n%15s%15s%15s\n","decimal","octal",
          "hexadecimal");

   for (i=0;i<=limit;i++)
      printf("%15d%15o%15x\n",i,i,i);
}

/*--------------------------------------------------------------*/

main()
{
   int limit;

   printf("A table showing Decimal - Octal -"
          " Hexadecimal Correspondence\n");
   printf("Input the table limit (in decimal, octal or"
          " hexadecimal form)\n");
   scanf("%i",&limit);
   output_table(limit);
}
```

Figure 2.8   Examples of the use of `printf()`

```
printf("%2d in hex= %X or %x and in octal is %o\n",
       15,15,15,15);
15 in hex= F or f and in octal is 17

printf("How do you like your reals? %f or %3.1f or %e\n",
       1.7,3.8,4.5);
How do you like your reals? 1.700000 or 3.8 or 4.500000e+00
```

Input using the scanf function

The function scanf() provides generalized input facilities corresponding to those for output provided by printf(). It has a similar general form:

scanf(< format string >, < argument list >);

the effect of which is to read one or more characters from the standard input device (typically, the user's keyboard), convert them into values according to the specification in the < format string >, and assign them to variables listed in the < argument list >. These arguments may be pointers (which are discussed in a later chapter), or simple variable names preceded by the character '&'. The presence of this character indicates that we are referring to the **address** of a program variable; of course, when we are reading a data value to be assigned to a variable, the address of the variable is required, so this prefix is essential. Again, we consider this further when we describe the parameter-passing mechanism of C in more detail.

As with printf(), the < format string > for scanf() can include both conversion specifications, prefixed by the '%' character, and other characters. Any characters other than space and tab included, apart from conversion specifications, are matched in sequence with non-space characters appearing in the input. When this facility is used it allows, for example, 'filler' text in the input to be checked for validity but otherwise ignored. 'White space' characters (space and tab) in the < format string > are matched with any number of white space characters in the corresponding position in the input. Thus, for example, the < format string > " %c" will read the next non-space character, after skipping an indefinite number of spaces.

Each conversion specification in the < format string > is used in sequence, to define a conversion of one or more characters in the input stream into a value of some type that is normally assigned to the next variable taken from the < argument list >. For example, in the call:

scanf("%d%f",&first,&second);

the conversion specification %d, which specifies a signed decimal integer, refers to the variable first, and %f, specifying a floating point number, refers to second. The effect of this call is to read from the input device a sequence of characters that together denote a signed integer, and assign its value to first, then to read further characters denoting a real number, whose value is assigned to second. The values in the input stream must be separated by 'white space' characters (space, tab, newline) which will be skipped over by scanf() when it looks for the next item of data.

The conversion specification codes used by scanf are listed in Figure 2.9.

%d	signed decimal integer
%i	signed integer
%o	unsigned octal integer
%u	unsigned decimal integer
%x	unsigned hexadecimal integer (using a,b,c,d,e,f)
%e,%f,%g	floating point notation
%c	character
%s	string
%p	pointer

Figure 2.9   Conversion specification codes for scanf()

Pointers and strings will be discussed more fully later. The other codes correspond to representations of the integer, real and character types; it is the responsibility of the programmer to ensure that these are matched correctly with the types of the corresponding variables in the argument list.

In most cases, 'white space' in the input stream will be used to terminate data representations, and otherwise ignored. However, the character-type conversion %c will read the next single character, including white space characters, and assign its ASCII code value to the corresponding argument. The %i code is used for integer representations that may include either octal (commencing with 0) or hexadecimal (commencing 0x or 0X).

As with printf() conversion codes, the codes used by scanf() may be qualified in various ways. The codes d,i,o,u and x may be prefixed with l or L to specify long integer types, or h to specify short integer, and e,f and g may be prefixed with l (for double) or L (for long double). An integer following the % symbol may be used to define the maximum number of characters to be read, in obtaining the value to be assigned. Finally, the character '*' in the conversion specification causes the assignment to be suppressed, allowing data to be read and skipped over where required.

Again the special pseudo-conversion code %n is used to cause the total number of characters read up to this point in the scanf() input to be assigned to the corresponding argument. The total number of *values* read and assigned is returned as the result of the call of scanf(), which may be assigned if required, and can be used to test for possible errors in the data stream.

Examples of the use of scanf():

```
int a,b;

scanf("%d%d",&a,&b);        ◄─────────── 3 4
printf("a= %d b=%d",a,b);   ───────────► a= 3 b= 4
```

```
int a,b;

scanf("%d,%d",&a,&b);       ◄─────────── 3 4
printf("a= %d b=%d",a,b);   ───────────► a= 3 b= 0
```

(The comma in the format string must be matched with a comma in the input sequence.)

```
int a,b;

scanf("%d,%d",&a,&b);       ◄─────────── 3,4
printf("a= %d b=%d",a,b);   ───────────► a= 3 b= 4
```

```
int a,b;

scanf("%2d%2d",&a,&b);      ◄─────────── 1234
printf("a= %d b=%d",a,b);   ───────────► a= 12 b= 34
```

```
char currency;
float value;

scanf("%f%c",&value,&currency);     ◄─────── 1.65        $
printf("%4.2f%c",value,currency);   ───────► 1.65
```

(The %c specification has resulted in a space character being read and assigned to currency.)

```
char currency;
float value;

scanf("%f %c",&value,&currency);      ◄──────  1.65      $
printf("%4.2f%c",value,currency);     ──────►  1.65$
```

(The space character preceding the %c specification has caused leading white space to be ignored before the character assignment is made.)

2.4   Simple control statements

The 'if' statement

The simplest form of the conditional statement in C is the if statement, which has the general form:

$$\begin{aligned}
&\text{if } (< condition >) \\
&\quad < statement1 >; \\
&\text{else} \\
&\quad < statement2 >;
\end{aligned}$$

The effect of this is that the $< condition >$ is evaluated to produce a boolean result (TRUE or FALSE); but recall that C has no explicit boolean type, so any integer-valued expression is interpreted as TRUE if its result is non-zero, or FALSE if it is zero. If the condition is TRUE, then the following statement, $< statement1 >$ is performed, otherwise $< statement2 >$ is performed. The else part of the conditional statement is optional; if this is omitted, the result of the statement is that $< statement1 >$ is performed if and only if the $< condition >$ is TRUE.

   Either or both of $< statement1 >$ and $< statement2 >$ can be a **compound statement**, that is, a sequence of statements enclosed within curly brackets.

Examples of 'if' statement:

```
if (character == '.') scanf( "%d",&fractional_part);
```

```
if (sex=='f' || sex=='F')
{
    num_women++;
    total_f_ages = total_f_ages + next_age;
}
else
{
    num_men++;
    total_m_ages = total_m_ages + next_age;
}

if (next%2) num_odd++; else num_even++;
```

Notice in the last example the use of an integer-valued expression (TRUE if non-zero). While this use is legitimate, this freedom in C can give rise to error. Note in particular that, in general, *any* expression (including an assignment-expression) has a result which, if it is an integer, could be interpreted as TRUE or FALSE. Thus, a common cause of error is to write (a=b) in place of (a==b); the former is an assignment-expression, but as it has a result equal to the value assigned, it is not flagged as an error by the compiler. For example, the conditional:

```
if (a=0) {...
```

is valid, and is always evaluated as FALSE, since the assignment-expression a=0 has the value 0, which is interpreted as FALSE.

Care must be taken over the use of boolean values in conditional statements; while ANSI C always represents the TRUE result of a logical expression by the value 1, it interprets *any* non-zero value, in an appropriate context, as the value TRUE. Suppose, for example, we define symbolic constants for the two boolean values, thus:

```
#define TRUE 1
#define FALSE 0
#define BOOL short
```

(the last #define has introduced a symbolic identifier BOOL that is identically equivalent to the reserved word short). Then we might go on to declare a variable flag of type BOOL (i.e. short) and use this in a condition of the form:

```
if (flag==TRUE) {...
```

Unfortunately, this is satisfied only when **flag** has the value 1; other non-zero values (which in C would normally be interpreted as TRUE) are not, in this case, acceptable.

The 'for' loop

There are a number of different forms of loop construction available in C, which will be described fully in Chapter 4. For the moment, we will introduce only one, the **for** statement, whose general form is:

   for ($<$ *initialization section* $>$; $<$ *condition section* $>$; $<$ *end section* $>$)
   $<$ *statement* $>$;

the effect of which is to repeat the $<$ *statement* $>$ that is the loop body (and which may be a **compound statement**) a number of times, depending on the **control section** which is contained in the brackets following **for**.

The control section, which is enclosed in brackets, comprises three parts, separated by semicolons:

1. The **initialization section**, which is performed once only, at the start of the loop.

2. The **condition section**, which specifies a condition to be evaluated prior to each traversal of the loop. The loop terminates when the condition has the result FALSE (0).

3. The **end section**, which is performed at the end of each loop traversal, i.e. after the execution of the loop body.

Note that the loop terminates *immediately* the condition is found to be FALSE, without further execution of either the loop body or the end section.

In the simplest case, each of the initialization, condition and end sections is a simple expression (which may, of course, be an assignment); for example:

```
/* Print a table of I and I squared */

printf("  I     I squared\n");
for (i=0;i<n;i++)
    printf("%d  %d\n",i,i*i);
```

In this case, the initialization section initializes the variable i to 0, and the end section increments it. The loop continues (for a positive-valued n) until i becomes equal to n.

Sometimes, it is useful to have sequences of statements as parts of the control section. We can do this by separating the statements by commas; thus:

```
/* Count the number of positive and the number
 * of negative numbers input
 */

for (num_pos=num_neg=0 , next=1; next!=0; )
{
    scanf("%d",&next);
    if (next>0) num_pos++;
    else if (next<0) num_neg++;
}
```

In this case, the initialization section comprises *two* assignment-expressions, separated by a comma, to perform two initializations. Notice also that there is no end section in this example. In fact, either or both of the initialization and end sections may be empty, but the separating semicolons must be present to maintain the structure of the control section as a whole.

The comma used to separate expressions in this example is in fact another **operator**, which is used to define a sequence of expression evaluations, the result of which is defined by the result of the last expression in the sequence. Its most common use, as in this example, is in a for loop in which the expressions in the sequence are typically assignments.

Also, in this example, the loop body was a compound statement. It is also possible for the loop body to be empty:

```
/* Read up to the next '.' or '?' */

for (scanf("%c",&next_char); next_char!='.' && next_char!='?';
         scanf("%c",&next_char))
{}
```

In this example, the repetition of the end section is sufficient. However, we have included the following pair of curly brackets, even though no loop body is present, to mark the extent of the loop construction. A simple

```
/* A set of exam marks are read in. The mark list
 * is terminated by a '*' character. All marks should
 * be in the range 0 to 100.
 *     e.g. 45 67 73 21 89 97 32 67 69 28 56 52 *
 * The following information is computed:
 *     the number of marks; the number passing;
 *     the number failing; and the average mark. */

#include <stdio.h>
#define PASS_MARK 45

main()
{
  int next_mark,read_in;
  int num_marks=0, num_fail=0, num_pass=0, accumulation=0;
  float average;
  char term;

  printf("Enter marks terminated by a '*' character\n");

  for (read_in = scanf("%d",&next_mark);
            read_in==1; read_in = scanf("%d",&next_mark))
  {
    if (next_mark<0 || next_mark>100)
        printf("\n***Data error*** Mark %d out of range\n",
                                                next_mark);
    else
    {
      ++num_marks;
      if (next_mark<PASS_MARK) ++num_fail; else ++num_pass;
      accumulation = accumulation+next_mark;
    }
  }

  scanf(" %c",&term);

  if (term != '*')
  {
    printf("\n***Illegal input char. code: %d char '%c'\n",
              term,term);
    exit(1);
  }
```

```
  else
  {
    if (num_marks==0)
    {
      printf("\n*** No marks entered! ***\n");
      exit(2);
    }
    else
    {
      average = accumulation/(float)num_marks;

      printf("There were %d marks in all\n",num_marks);
      printf("%d passed and %d failed\n",num_pass,num_fail);
      printf("The average mark was %5.2f\n",average);
    }
  }
}
```

Figure 2.10   A program to calculate examination statistics

semicolon would have been sufficient for this purpose, but we prefer the style we have used as it indicates more clearly the absence of a loop body.

Figure 2.10 gives a final program example to illustrate the use of the **for** loop, **if** statements, and a number of other program features we have introduced in this chapter. Notice in particular the form of the loop control section:

```
for (read_in=scanf("%d",&next_mark);
          read_in==1;read_in=scanf("%d",&next_mark))
```

which causes the loop to continue as each **next_mark** is read in turn, until the call of **scanf()** fails to read a number (as happens when the terminating character is encountered). In this event, **scanf()** returns the value 0, causing the loop condition to fail and the loop to be terminated. Note also the use of a **cast** in the statement:

```
average=accumulation/(float)num_marks;
```

2.5   Exercises

1. Which of the following names are legal as variable names?
   MaxiMum   class-size   Freds's_house
   large_1   1more   happy hour

2. Write a program to average a set of real numbers that are entered at the keyboard. The character '*' is typed directly following the last number to indicate the end of the data (e.g. 72.56*).

3. Write a function that, when given the time of day in London, prints out the equivalent time in New York (-5 hours) and in Tokyo (+9 hours). The time is input as a real number (e.g. 21.30 represents 9.30pm).

4. Write a program that determines whether three sides, whose lengths are input, can form a triangle. (A triangle can be formed if the sum of two sides is greater than the third.)

5. Write a program to calculate the average heights of both men and women from a population sample. Data for each person consists of firstly either 'M' (or 'm'), 'F' (or 'f') to indicate the gender of the person followed by their height in metres. Data is terminated by '*'.

6. Write a program to print out a neat table of values showing the circumference and area of a circle for radii ranging from 1cm to 15cm in intervals of 1cm, and from 15cm to 50cm in intervals of 5cm. Print out the results to three decimal places. (Pi = 3.14159)

7. Write a function to test if a number has either 3 or 5 as a factor. Return TRUE (the value 1) if 3 or 5 is a factor, otherwise return FALSE (the value 0). Use your function to compute how many integers in the range 0 to 9999 have 3 or 5 as a factor.

8. Write a program to count how many spaces, capital letters, lower case letters, digits and punctuation marks there are in a sentence that is typed in at the keyboard. You can assume that a full stop terminates the sentence and that the punctuation marks are restricted to the following:
   ,   ?   !   :   ;

9. Write a function that returns its character argument with even parity set.

Chapter 3

Arrays and pointers

3.1 Arrays in C

As well as the basic scalar types `int`, `float` and so on, which were introduced in the previous chapter, it is also possible in C to declare variables that are multiples of these values. An **array** in C is an ordered set of data objects, each of which is of the same type. The general form of an array declaration is:

$$< type > < name > [< number\ of\ elements >]$$

For example:

```
int numbers[10];
```

Declarations of arrays can occur in the same way as other declarations, i.e. globally or locally, and the same rules apply for forming names. The $< number\ of\ elements >$ is an integer constant or an integer-valued expression, the terms of which are constants.

The effect of the example declaration is to set aside an array of 10 elements, each of which is of type `int`. The elements are stored consecutively, and may be referred to by applying an index to the array name; for example, the statement:

```
numbers[5] = 1;
```

assigns the value 1 to element 5 of the array `numbers`. In C, the indexes of an array are always numbered from 0, so the elements of the example array are `numbers[0]`,`numbers[1]`,`numbers[2]`...`numbers[9]`. However, C compilers will not check that an array index is within the bounds defined

```
/*
 * This example counts how many numbers in a data set fall
 * in each of the 10 ranges, 0-9, 10-19,...90-99.
 * The data is terminated by the first -ve number entered.
 */

#include <stdio.h>

main()
{
  int counts[10]; /* to hold the number in each range */
  int next;       /* holds next number entered */
  int i;          /* used as a loop counter */

  for (i=0;i<10;i++) counts[i]=0;

  printf("Enter data terminated by a -ve value.\n");

  for (scanf("%d",&next); next>=0; scanf("%d",&next))
     if (next<100) counts[next/10]++;
     else printf ("data error %d out of range\n",next);

  for (i=0;i<10;i++)
     printf("%d in the range %2d-%2d\n",
                                counts[i],i*10,i*10+9);
}
```

An example run:

```
Enter data terminated by a -ve value.
23 42 67 12 56 23 89 24 34 23 91 -1
0 in the range  0- 9
1 in the range 10-19
4 in the range 20-29
1 in the range 30-39
1 in the range 40-49
1 in the range 50-59
1 in the range 60-69
0 in the range 70-79
1 in the range 80-89
1 in the range 90-99
```

Figure 3.1   Example of the use of an array

by the declaration, so a reference to **numbers[10]**, which would almost certainly lead to an error, would not be flagged by the compiler.

Figure 3.1 illustrates a simple application of an array. Note that the index used when referring to an array element may, in general, be any integer-valued expression. Notice also the loop used to initialize the array:

```
for (i=0;i<10;i++) counts[i]=0;
```

Common errors in this case are to start the loop from **i=1**, or to continue until **i==10**.

Storage of arrays

As we have mentioned, a declaration of an array sets aside *consecutive* memory locations to contain its elements. In most high-level programming languages, the way in which arrays and other data structures are represented internally is not relevant; however, because C allows us to manipulate machine **addresses** in ways that are not permitted in higher-level languages, it often becomes important to know these details.

Consider, for example, the program illustrated in Figure 3.2, which we have shown in a line-numbered listing produced by the hypothetical debugging system introduced in Chapter 1.

An allocation of memory space to store the variable **i**, and the arrays **array** and **real**, is shown in Figure 3.3; this is a **local** memory allocation, as the declarations take place *inside* the function **main()**. Some details of this are machine-dependent, such as, for example, the fact that the allocation of memory space is in descending order of addresses (so that the last declaration, i.e. variable **i**, has the lowest-numbered address). The actual addresses shown (in hexadecimal notation) at the right of the diagram are for illustration only, of course.

We can inspect this allocation using our debugging system. Suppose that we do this following a breakpoint at line 18:

> *? show &i*
> *0xffeffccc*

The notation **&***i* indicates that we want to display not the value of **i**, but the address of the location used for **i**. As we shall see, this is a convention that is also used within programs written in C. When, however, we give the command:

```
 1: /* Looking at arrays in memory */
 2: #include <stdio.h>
 3:
 4: main()
 5: {
 6:     int array[10];
 7:     double real[10];
 8:     int i;
 9:     for (i=0;i<10;i++)
10:     {
11:         array[i]=i;
12:         real[i]=i*0.1;
13:     }
14:     printf("That's all\n");
15: }
```

Figure 3.2   Simple arrays

? show array
0xffeffd20

we again get the address of the array displayed (in hexadecimal form). This is because, in C, the array name in its unsubscripted form stands for the address of the array as a whole (i.e. the address of its first element). Applying a subscript, or index, to the array name allows us to inspect the values of individual elements:

? show array[0]
0xffeffd20   0
? next
0xffeffd24   1

(The *next* command, in this context, displays the next element of the array in sequence.)

? show array[9]
0xffeffd44   9
? next
0xffeffd48   0

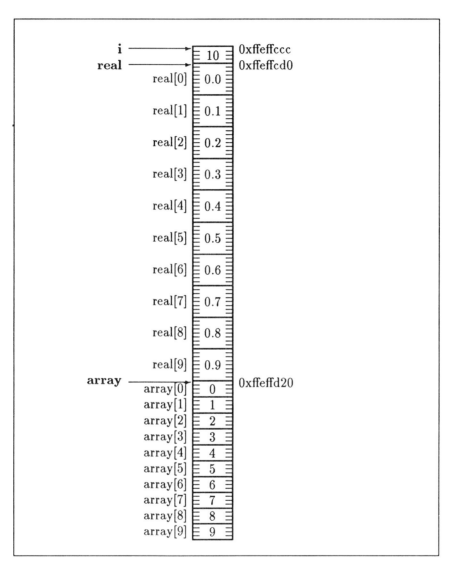

Figure 3.3   The allocation of local memory for Figure 3.2

(Notice that if we 'step off the end' of the array, we will find an undefined value—in this case, 0.)

```
? show real[0]
0xffeffcd0     0
? show real[9]
0xffeffd18     0.9
? next
0xffeffd20     4.94065645841247e-324
```

(Again, stepping off the end of the array `real` has located an arbitrary value. In this case, the value obtained is taken from the start of the adjacent array (i.e. `array`). However, because the types of the two arrays are different, in this context the value displayed is in fact constructed from the bit-patterns used for the first *two* elements of `array`.)

You may wish to examine the program of Figure 3.2 using the debugging system available to you. Knowing how arrays and other variables are represented in the memory is not always necessary, of course, but can sometimes be important in a language like C that allows the programmer unusual freedom to reference the program's address space in unorthodox (and error-prone!) ways.

Initialization of arrays

When an array is declared, it is possible to initialize it to a set of constant values, by appending an assignment to the declaration. Thus, for example:

```
int counts[5] = {10,20,30,40,50};
```

When this form of declaration is used, the size of the array may be omitted from within the square brackets, and is inferred from the number of elements in the set of initialization values. If the number of elements is defined explicitly, then the number of initialization values must be no greater than this, or an error will ensue. If the number of values provided is less than the defined size of the array, then the undefined (high-index) array elements are initialized to 0 (in the case of a global declaration) or otherwise remain undefined. In all cases the terms in the set of initialization values must be constants, or expressions made up of constants only.

Strings, which we have encountered briefly previously, are in fact implemented in C as arrays of characters. For this special case, a different

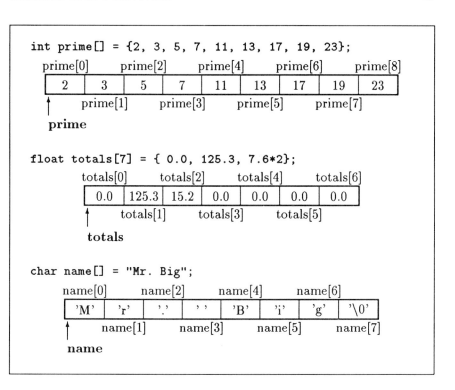

Figure 3.4   Examples of array initializations

form of array initialization is permitted, in which the initialization values are expressed as a string constant. Note, however, that in this case a null character is implied as a string terminator, and this is assigned as the last element of the initialized array.

Figure 3.4 illustrates some examples of array initializations, using the familiar pictorial convention of a box to represent a machine location, the value of which is written inside.

3.2   Pointers

We have previously referred to the fact that C, unlike most high-level languages, allows the manipulation of machine addresses as program values. We can do this by declaring variables which are of **pointer** types. For example, the declaration:

```
int *iptr;
```

declares a variable (iptr) whose type is int *, which we may read as 'pointer to integer'. In general, a pointer declaration takes the form:

$$< type > *< name >;$$

where the $< type >$ defines the data type of the objects to which the variable may refer. In the example, the value assigned to the variable iptr should be the address of a memory location that is used to contain a value of type int.

Observe that it is the asterisk prefix to the variable name, in the declaration, that identifies it as a pointer variable. Thus, for example, the declaration:

```
int *iptr,count;
```

declares two variables, only one of which (iptr) is of the pointer type int *; the other, count, is a simple int variable.

We can give a value to a pointer variable by assigning to it the address of another variable. Thus, if num1 is a variable of type float, and ptr is of type float *, then the assignment:

```
ptr = &num1;
```

will assign to ptr the address of num1; we may now say that ptr 'points to' num1. The & symbol here represents a monadic operator, the effect of which is to obtain the memory address of its operand; naturally, the operand must be something which has an identifiable memory address, such as a variable name.

Notice that the asterisk prefix that is used in the declaration of a pointer variable is not itself part of the variable name. When an asterisk is used to prefix the name of a pointer variable in an expression, it has a different significance. It is another monadic operator, the effect of which is to **dereference** its operand; that is to say, it uses the contents of the pointer variable to reference the location to which it points.

Figure 3.5 illustrates the effects of the & (address of) and * (contents of) operators. The pointer variable ptr is initially assigned to point to the location used for the variable num1. Then the assignment:

```
num2 = *ptr + 5;
```

obtains the value contained in this location (i.e. 15.7), adds 5 to it, and assigns the result to num2. The subsequent assignment:

```
*ptr = 6.5;
```

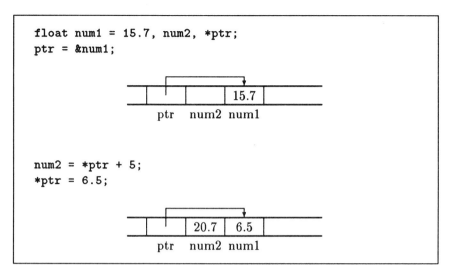

Figure 3.5   Example of the use of the **&** and ***** operators

has the effect of assigning, not to the variable ptr itself, but to the location to which ptr points, i.e. the variable num1.

The two operators, **&** and *****, are complementary; **&** delivers the address of a simple variable, while ***** dereferences a pointer variable to obtain the simple variable to which it points. The freedom with which C allows us to manipulate addresses as pointers can, of course, lead to serious errors. Beware in particular the dangers of using unallocated pointers; if we make an assignment such as:

$$*ptr = 10;$$

before the pointer variable ptr has been assigned to point to a known location, then the effect will be to make a change to some undefined memory location. We also need to take consideration of the **storage class** of a value to which a pointer refers. If we make an assignment:

$$ptr = \&localvar;$$

which sets ptr to point to a variable which is local to a function, then after the function has terminated we may be left with a 'dangling reference', i.e. a pointer to a location which is no longer allocated.

```
/*
 * Program to show how pointers can be used to access arrays.
 */

#include <stdio.h>

int powers[] = {1, 4, 9, 16, 25, 36};

main()
{
    int *ptr = powers;

    printf("addr %lx contains %d\n",
        ptr,*ptr);  ─────────────────────→ addr 3000 contains 1


    ptr = ptr+4;

    printf("addr %lx contains %d\n",
        ptr,*ptr);  ─────────────────────→ addr 3010 contains 25


}
```

Figure 3.6   Accessing arrays with pointers

Arithmetic with pointers

The only permissible arithmetic operations on variables of pointer type
are addition and subtraction using the diadic operators + and -, and the
increment and decrement operators ++ and --. In almost all cases, the
term that is added to or subtracted from a pointer variable must itself be
a simple integer, which will be automatically scaled to the size appropriate
for the data type to which the pointer refers. Thus, if the size of an int
representation is 32 bits (4 bytes), incrementation of a variable of type
int * in fact adds 4 to the pointer-value, so that the pointer is increased
to point to the next adjacent integer-storage location in memory.

   It is *not*, in general, legal to add or subtract two pointer variables. The
only exception is that two pointers which both refer to elements of the same
array may be subtracted to obtain a value that is equal to the number of

array elements separating them. Pointers to elements of the same array may also be compared, and any pointer variable can be compared to zero.

Figure 3.6 gives a simple illustration of the use of pointer arithmetic, and the effect of scaling to produce the address required from an expression. Notice also from this example that the declaration:

```
int *ptr = powers;
```

both declares and initializes the variable **ptr**. The value assigned is the address of the array **powers** (that is, the address of its first element). In this case we do *not* require to use the **&** operator, as the unsubscripted name of an array is itself used to denote the (constant) address of the array.

Precedence of pointer operators

The ***** and **&** operators are both monadic, and have the same precedence as other monadic operators. Evaluation of sequences of these operators takes place in right-to-left order; that is, an operator associates with its adjacent operand. Occasionally, some care is needed to ensure that the expected effects ensue in these cases. Consider the short program of Figure 3.7. The initial declaration and assignment:

```
int *ptr = vec
```

assigns to **ptr** the address of the array **vec**. Then, the assignment:

```
fetched = *ptr++;
```

will *first* apply the 'contents of' operator (*****) to **ptr**, to obtain the value of the first element of the array; it is this value which is assigned to the variable **fetched**. Because the **++** operator is being used in its postincrement form, the incrementation will not take effect until after this value has been obtained. Note also, however, that the incrementation is applied to the *pointer* value, with the effect that **ptr** will, after the assignment, point to the second element of the array. Had we wished to increment the contents of the array, rather than the pointer, then we would have had to write:

```
fetched = (*ptr)++;
```

which again first assigns the value of the first element of the array to **fetched**, and then increments this value in the store.

It is clear that had the assignment been written:

```
fetched = *++ptr;
```

```
/*
 * This program illustrates how to fetch the contents of
 * a pointer and then increment the pointer
 */

#include <stdio.h>

int vec [] = {1,10,20,30,40};

main()
{
    int *ptr = vec, fetched = 0;

    printf("ptr addr is %lx has contents %d, fetched = %d\n",
           ptr,*ptr,fetched);

    fetched = *ptr++;

    printf("ptr addr is %lx has contents %d, fetched = %d\n",
           ptr,*ptr,fetched);
}
```

Figure 3.7   Fetching and incrementing a pointer

the effect would have been to first increment the pointer, making it point
to the second element of the array, and then to obtain this value for assignment. Similarly, the assignment:

$$\text{fetched = ++*ptr;}$$

will first obtain the contents of the pointer (i.e. the first element of the
array), and then increment this value in the memory before making the
assignment. These two cases both illustrate the right-to-left associativity
of the pair of monadic operators.

The results of these operations on pointer variables are depicted graph-
ically in Figure 3.8. Readers may care to confirm these effects by trying
out the program of Figure 3.7 with these and other variations.

One occasional source of error associated with the use of the * operator
may be mentioned here. The statement:

$$\text{a= x/*ptr;}$$

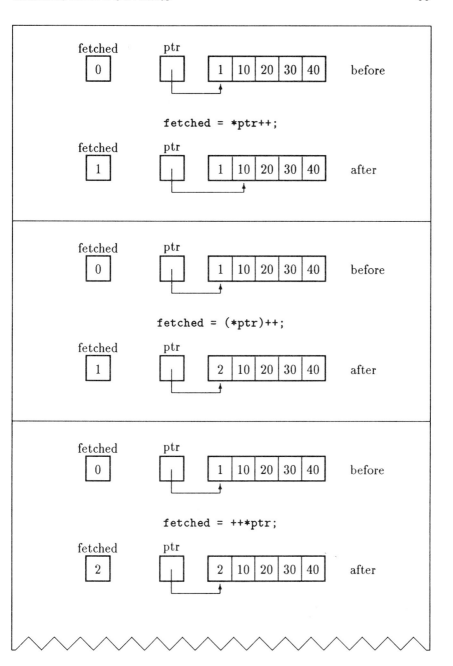

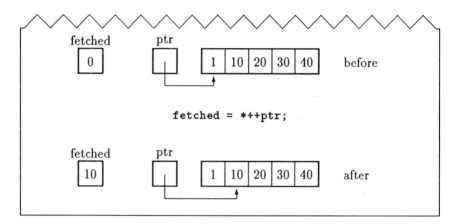

Figure 3.8   Combining the 'contents of' and 'increment' operators

intended to divide **x** by the value obtained from the contents of **ptr**, will not in fact have this effect. This is because the sequence **/*** will be interpreted as the start of a comment. To avoid this problem, we must write:

$$a= x/ *ptr;$$

i.e. separating the **/** and ***** symbols with a space.

3.3   Parameter passing

Now that we have introduced pointer variables, we are better able to describe the mechanisms involved when a call of a function is made, involving the passing of parameters to the function. Recall from our introduction to this topic in Section 2.1 that the declaration of a function is headed by a specification of its **formal parameters**; for example, the function header:

$$int \; min(int \; first,int \; second)$$

declares the integer variables **first** and **second** as formal parameters of the function **min()**. When a call of the function is made, e.g.:

$$result = min(a,b)$$

the actual parameters **a** and **b** are used to provide values for the formal parameters that are used when the function is executed. The effect is that the actual parameters (which may, of course, be expressions) are evaluated at the point of call and their values are assigned, in order, to provide initial values for the formal parameters at the start of the function's execution. The formal parameters behave as if they were local variables declared at the start of the function body and assigned these initial values. Thus, a change to the value of a formal parameter within the body of the function is quite legal, but does not affect the value of the actual parameter in the calling environment.

This **call-by-value** parameter-passing mechanism is the only one used in C for all kinds of functions and parameter types. We can, however, reproduce the effect of **call-by-reference** with the use of pointer variables as parameters. If we declare the formal parameter to be of a pointer type, and if the actual parameter supplied is itself a pointer (i.e. the address of a variable), then the **value** passed will be this address. It is then possible, within the function body, to use this address (pointer) to examine and change the value of the variable referred to in the calling environment.

Figure 3.9 illustrates the distinction between the normal call-by-value mechanism, and the use of this mechanism with pointer variables to emulate call-by-reference. In the first case, the assignment:

$$y = 1;$$

within the function body has a purely local effect, and does not change the value of the corresponding actual parameter **x**. In the second case, however, the assignment:

$$*y = 1;$$

assigns to the 'contents of' the pointer variable **y**, i.e. to the location pointed to by this parameter. As the value passed to **y** is the address of **x** (**&x**), the assignment has the effect of assigning to **x**.

Figure 3.10 illustrates the way in which memory is likely to be allocated when the two calls are made (with illustrative values for machine addresses, expressed in hexadecimal form). In the first case, the value (5) of the actual parameter **x** is assigned as the initial value of the formal parameter **y**. We have also shown the allocation of memory to store the return address of the function and a frame pointer to the calling environment. In the second case, the value assigned to **y** is the address of the actual parameter.

Arrays as parameters

The call-by-value mechanism of C does not allow us to pass as an actual parameter the set of elements of an array. If we define the parameter to be of pointer type, however, we can pass the address of the array as the actual parameter, and in this way obtain access to the elements of the array.

```
/* Functions illustrating the difference between
 * call by value and call by reference */
#include <stdio.h>

void call_by_value(int y)
{ y = 1; }

/*--------------------------------------------------------*/

void call_by_reference(int *y)
{ *y = 1; }

/*--------------------------------------------------------*/

main()
{
    int x=5;
    printf("original x= %d\n",x);

    call_by_value(x);
    printf("x should be the same as before x = %d\n",x);

    call_by_reference(&x);
    printf("x should have changed x= %d\n",x);
}
```

Figure 3.9   Call-by-value and call-by-reference

Figure 3.11 illustrates this mechanism. The function **sum()** has a formal
parameter **data** which is of type **int** ∗. When this function is called from
within **main()**, the actual parameter is the address of the array **values**
(note, again, that the use of the unsubscripted name of the array denotes
its address). Within the function, the expression:

$$*(data+i)$$

obtains the **contents** of the ith element of the actual array; recall that the
array elements are numbered from 0, and that the addition to the value
of the pointer **data** is scaled to the size of the elements. The effect of the
loop used in the function **sum()** is to add together the elements of the array

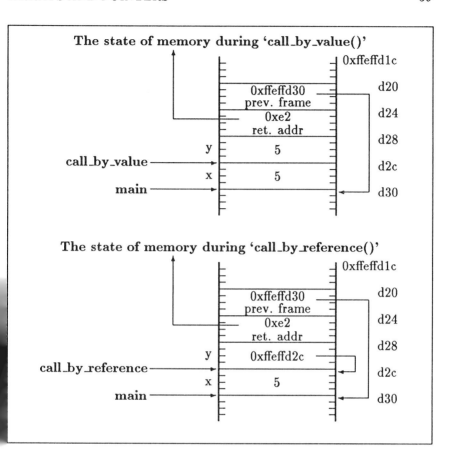

Figure 3.10   Memory allocation for functions in Figure 3.9

values; the 'loop counter' i is initialized to 0 at the start of the loop, and incremented at the end of each traversal of the loop.

Notice also that the function **sum()** uses a second parameter to define the size of (number of elements in) the array. Because the actual parameter **values** is simply the address of the array—i.e. the address of its first element—there is no automatic way in which the function can know the size of the array. Consequently, passing the size as a second parameter is a commonly-used device.

In the program of Figure 3.11, and similar examples, the *value* of the pointer parameter is being used as a *reference* to the array, which remains in the memory in its original locations (and may be altered by using this

```
/*
 * Program to illustrate the passing of
 * arrays to functions.
 */

#include <stdio.h>
#define SIZE 5

/*
 * 'Sum' adds up the elements of an array.
 * 'data' is a pointer to the array to be used.
 * 'num_items' is the number of elements in the array.
 */

int sum(int *data, int num_items)
{
    int total, i;

    for (i=total=0;i<num_items;i++) total = total + *(data+i);

    return total;
}

/*----------------------------------------------------------*/

main()
{
    int values[SIZE], i;

    for (i=0;i<SIZE;i++) values[i]=i;

    printf("total =%d\n",sum(values,SIZE));
}
```

Figure 3.11   A function with an array parameter

pointer to change its elements). Figure 3.12 illustrates a possible layout of the array and other information in the memory, using, again, illustrative values for the addresses of locations. You may like to compare this with the organization you find on the system you are using; to do this, use the debugging system to set a breakpoint on the **return** statement of **sum()**, and then inspect the addresses and values of the variables and array elements concerned.

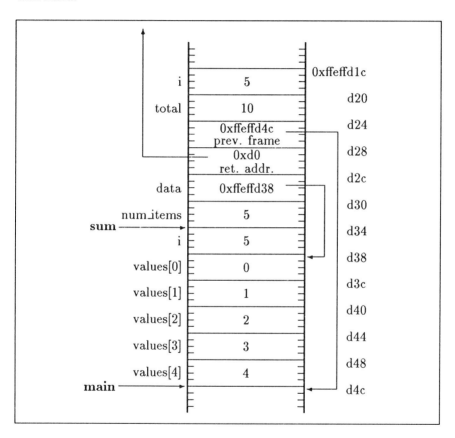

Figure 3.12 The state of memory just prior to the return from 'sum()'

The form of loop used in the function **sum** in Figure 3.11 is only one of a number of possible ways in which the same effects could be obtained. Figure 3.13 illustrates some alternatives, in each of which the summation of the array elements is included as part of the 'end section' of the loop control section, rather than within the body of the loop. Notice in particular the

```
/*
 * Post increment 'i' when data is accessed
 */
int sum(int *data, int num_items)
{
    int total,i;

    for (i=total=0; i<num_items; total=total + *(data+i++)){}

    return total;
}
```

```
/*
 * Treat data as an array (i.e. index a pointer).
 */
int sum(int *data, int num_items)
{
    int total,i;

    for (i=total=0; i<num_items; total = total+data[i++] ){}

    return total;
}
```

```
/*
 * Step through the array by incrementing the pointer.
 */
int sum(int *data,int num_items)
{
    int total,i;

    for (i=total=0; i<num_items; total=total + *data++,i++){}

    return total;
}
```

Figure 3.13   Alternative ways of writing 'sum.c'

second alternative in Figure 3.13, in which the pointer variable **data** is being used as if it were an array name. In C, an index can be applied (using the square brackets notation) to any pointer-value (of which an array name, which is a *constant* pointer, is just a special case).

This is probably the most frequently used method of array indexing, following as it does the conventions used in most other languages. It cannot be applied in the same way to arrays of two or more dimensions (which we will discuss shortly), so many experienced C programmers prefer to use the third alternative, in which the value of the pointer variable is being incremented as the loop proceeds. Because the value of the pointer is itself the actual parameter, incrementing this value causes it to point in turn to successive elements of the array.

In these examples, we have declared the formal parameter **data** to be of type **int *** because its value will be the address of an array. We could in fact have made this explicit by using an alternative form of declaration, thus:

```
int sum(int data[],int num_items)
```

In this case, the parameter **data** is declared to be of type 'array of integer' but, because the array name always denotes the address of the array, this form is in fact exactly equivalent to the declaration in which **data** is defined to be of pointer type.

Function prototypes

A rather more substantial program making use of an array parameter to a function is shown as Figure 3.14. In this example, the **main()** function reads a single number, and then calls the function **find_number** to determine whether the given number is present in a list of numbers stored as the array **data**.

In this program, unlike the earlier program examples we have shown, the declaration of the subsidiary function **find_number()** *follows* rather than precedes the declaration of **main()**. As a result, the call of **find_number()** from within **main()** is a **forward reference**. While this kind of forward reference is not illegal in C, it can sometimes give rise to problems. In particular, when a call of a function that has not been declared is first encountered, the compiler will make certain assumptions about the types of the parameters and the result of the function, which may not precisely conform to the actual definition of the function when it is made.

To overcome these problems, the function **find_number()** in Figure 3.14 has been introduced, before the declaration of **main()**, in the form of a **function prototype**:

```
/* An example of passing an array to a function.
 * The array is terminated by a zero element. */

#include <stdio.h>
#define NOT_FOUND -1

int data[]={71,45,67,-5,34,0};

/* A function prototype: specifies the data types of the
 * result and arguments of the function. */
int find_number(int *,int);

main()
{
  int num,position;
  printf("Enter the number to be searched for ");
  scanf("%d",&num);

  if ((position=find_number(data,num))>=0)
      printf("number found at position %d\n",position);
  else printf("number not in the array\n");
}
/*----------------------------------------------------------*/

/* find_number searches 'list' for 'key'.
 * 'list' is a ptr to a 0 terminated integer array.
 * 'key' should be an integer value.
 * RETURNS:-ve value => key not found.
 *          0 or +ve value => the index where found.
 */
int find_number(int *list,int key)
{
   int found,i;
   for (i=0,found=NOT_FOUND; *list !=0 && *list != key;
                                          i++,list++){}
   if (*list == key) found = i;
   return found;
}
```

Figure 3.14   A second example of passing an array to a function

```
int find_number(int *,int);
```

The function prototype defines the name of the function, and the types of its result and parameters, without the need to declare formal parameter names or to define the body of the function. This preliminary function declaration can then be made globally, avoiding the need for the compiler to infer a function declaration from the context of a function call.

In passing, it is worth noting the use of a special element value (in this case, 0) to mark the effective end of the array **data** used in this program. This device obviates the need to pass a parameter defining the size of the array; instead, the loop in **find_number** continues while *list != 0 (i.e. while the contents of the location referenced by the array pointer **list** are non-zero). The pointer-type parameter **list** is initialized, at the function call, to the address of the actual parameter, which is the array **data**, and is incremented repeatedly in the end section of the loop.

Again, it may be instructive to examine the memory allocation used in this program. Figure 3.15 illustrates the relationship between the parameters **list** and **key**, and the array **data** (with, again, arbitrary location addresses shown for illustration).

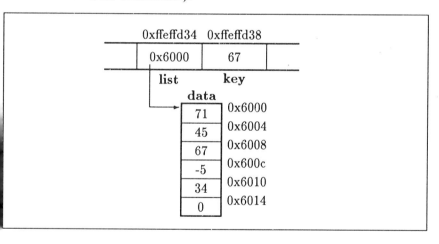

Figure 3.15   Memory allocation for 'find_number()'

In Figure 3.16, we show how our debugging system could be used to uncover these details. A line-numbered listing of part of the program is followed by a sequence of instructions to the debugger to execute the program and inspect memory addresses and values. Repeating this exercise, using the debugging system that is available to you, may help clarify the mechanisms involved in the use of pointers and parameters in C.

```
25: /* find_number searches 'list' for 'key'.
26:  * 'list' is a ptr to a 0 terminated integer array.
27:  * 'key' should be an integer value.
28:  * RETURNS:-ve value => key not found.
29:  *          0 or +ve value => index where found.
30:  */
31: int find_number(int *list,int key)
32: {
33:     int found,i;
34:     for (i=0,found=NOT_FOUND; *list !=0 && *list != key;
35:                                      i++,list++){}
36:     if (*list == key) found = i;
37:     return found;
38: }
```

```
? setbreakpoint 34
? run
Enter the number to be searched for   67
breakpoint at line 34
? show &key
0xffeffd38
? show key
67
? show &list
0xffeffd34
? show list
0x6000
? show *list
ox6000    71
? next
ox6004    45
? next
ox6008    67
? next
ox600c    -5
? next
ox6010    34
? next
ox6014    0
```

Figure 3.16   Inspection of program using debugging system

Command-line arguments

In the very first program we looked at (Figure 1.1), the topic of command-line arguments was introduced. We are now able to explain this more completely. In that program, **main()** received two parameters:

$$\texttt{main(int argc,char *argv[])}$$

The first of these, **argc**, is a simple parameter of type **int**. When, as in this case, the *actual* parameter is a 'command-line argument'—that is, the function is invoked by a command to perform the program, rather than by an internal call—the value assigned to **argc** will be the number of distinct words in the command line (including the command name itself).

The type of the second parameter deserves careful examination. We know that a declaration of the form:

$$\texttt{char aa[];}$$

would introduce an array **aa**, the elements of which are of type **char**. In this case however, the formal parameter is defined by the declaration:

$$\texttt{char *argv[]}$$

which denotes an array the elements of which are of type **char** *, i.e. which are themselves pointers. In this context, the actual parameter is an array the elements of which point to strings representing the words in the command line.

Consider, for example, a function **main()**, with this parameter list, which is the main function of a route-finding program. The program is invoked by the command:

$ route Liverpool London

As a result of this call, **argc** will now have the value 3, representing the three words on the command line, and **argv** will contain the address of an array the elements of which are the addresses of the three command-line words (Figure 3.17). The pointer **argv** could be used in a number of ways to refer to these strings; for example:

```
argv[0]     /* points to the program name "route" */

argv[1]     /* points to the 1st argument "Liverpool" */

argv[2]     /* points to the 2nd argument "London" */
```

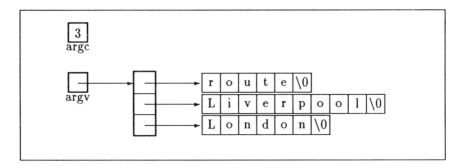

Figure 3.17   Command-line arguments

```
*argv        /* will initially point to "route" */

*argv[2]     /* will access the character 'u' */

*++argv      /* will produce a pointer to "Liverpool" */
```

In this example, `argv` is a pointer to an array whose elements are themselves pointers to arrays. This is an example of a **two-dimensional** array structure; these and other array forms are discussed in the next section.

3.4   Further array constructions

Dynamic arrays and memory allocation

The arrays we have described so far have been **static** structures, the sizes of which are defined by declaration and fixed when the program is compiled; recall that the number of elements defined in the array declaration must be a **constant** expression. In real programming problems, however, and particularly for the systems programming problems for which C is particularly suited, there is very often a need to manage arrays and other structures whose dimensions are determined dynamically when the program is executed. C helps us to do this by the provision of two standard library functions, which are available in all complete ANSI C implementations. The `malloc()` function obtains a block of memory, the size of which may be determined at run-time, and the `free()` function may be used to release unwanted areas of memory. Because of the freedom which C offers to reference memory through pointer variables, these functions are sufficient to allow us to implement many kinds of dynamic memory structures.

The malloc() and free() functions

The library function `malloc()` obtains an allocation of memory the size (in bytes) of which is defined by its parameter. The **type** of this parameter is system-dependent, but will usually be **int** or **unsigned int**. The function returns as its result the address of the block of memory allocated. Thus, if we declare a variable:

<code>int *ptr;</code>

and then perform the assignment:

<code>ptr = malloc(10);</code>

the effect will be to allocate a previously unused area of memory of size 10 bytes and assign its address to the pointer `ptr` (Figure 3.18).

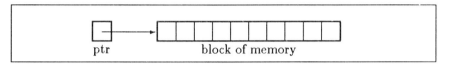

Figure 3.18 Result of the statement `ptr = malloc(10)`

Of course, in real use the actual parameter is usually a variable or expression, enabling us to obtain an allocation of memory the size of which is determined dynamically. Often we will want to express this size in terms of elements other than bytes; to help us do this, C provides a monadic operator **sizeof** which obtains the number of bytes required to store an element of any particular type. For example:

```
int n,m; float f;

n = sizeof(f);      /* obtains the number of bytes required
                       for the variable f */
m = sizeof(double); /* obtains the number of bytes required
                       to store a variable of type double */
```

The result returned by the **sizeof** operator is of the type, `size_t`, which is specified for the parameter of `malloc()`. In practice, as in these examples, we can safely assign its value to a variable of type **int**.

Note that the result returned by a call of `malloc()` is a pointer to the area of memory allocated. The type of this result is defined to be **void ***, which is a generic pointer type used in C to describe a pointer to any data type. The effect is that we can assign the result of `malloc()` to any type of pointer variable, without the need to apply a cast to force it to the required type.

The library function `free()` reverses the effect of a call of `malloc()`. Its parameter should be a pointer to a memory area previously allocated through `malloc()`, which is released for potential reuse by the call of `free()`. The use of `free()` with a parameter that is *not* the address of a memory block obtained by using `malloc()` will produce undefined and possibly disastrous results.

Figure 3.19 demonstrates the use of these functions in a simple program. Notice that the start of the program includes the line:

```
#include <stdlib.h>
```

which tells the compiler that the program contains calls of routines (in this case `malloc()` and `free()`) that are contained in the library referenced by *stdlib.h*; this is in addition to the standard input and output routines referenced by *stdio.h*. *stdlib.h* and *stdio.h* are in fact **header files** which contain **function prototypes** for the library functions required. We explain this more fully in Chapter 5.

The program reads a value, `num`, and then uses the expression:

```
sizeof(float)*num
```

to define the number of bytes required to store an array of `num` elements, each of which is of type `float`. The call of `malloc()` with this argument should return the address of an area of this size. If insufficient space is available for allocation, `malloc()` will return a null (zero-valued) pointer. It is usually necessary to test for this; in Figure 3.19, if the allocation fails, the program prints an appropriate message, and then calls another library function, `exit()`. This function is used when, as in this case, we wish to invoke a premature termination of the program. In simple cases, the argument of `exit()` is redundant, but it is conventional to use `exit(0)` to signify successful termination, and non-zero values to define alternative cases. The value is returned to the program calling environment, where it may be available in system-dependent ways.

The area of memory obtained by `malloc()` initially contains undefined values; the program of Figure 3.19 proceeds to assign an array of `float` values within this area and would (in a more complete example) be expected to go on to make some use of this array before releasing the area with a call of `free()`.

```
/*
 * This program illustrates the use of malloc()
 */

#include <stdio.h>
#include <stdlib.h>

#define NULL 0

main()
{
    int num,i;
    float *ptr, *next;

    printf("How many reals do I need to house? ");
    scanf("%d",&num);

    ptr = malloc(sizeof(float)*num);

    if (ptr==NULL)
    {
        printf("malloc() unable to meet request\n");
        exit(1);
    }

    printf("Enter the %d reals\n",num);
    next = ptr;
    for (i=0;i<num;i++) scanf("%f",next++);

    /* Presumably one would use the array for
     * some purpose now
     */

    free(ptr);
}
```

Figure 3.19   Using malloc()

Multi-dimensional arrays

The structure of a two-dimensional array was briefly touched on in the previous section, when we discussed command-line arguments. In general, as in that case, a two-dimensional array in C takes the form of an array of one-dimensional arrays. If we think of a one-dimensional array as a row of memory cells, thus:

row

then we can think of a two-dimensional array as an array of rows:

row[0]

row[1]

row[2]

We could declare an array of this form using the declaration:

int a[3][5];

which defines an array of three 'rows', each of which has five elements (or 'columns'). Of course, the concept of rows and columns is an interpretation we place on the memory structure used; in fact, the actual memory allocation arising from this declaration will store the elements in sequence, thus:

row[0]   row[1]   row[2]

In general, the declaration of a two-dimensional array takes the form:

$< type >< name > [< size\ of\ 1st\ dimension >]\ [< size\ of\ 2nd\ dimension >]$

where the size of the first dimension specifies the number of 'rows', leading to a row-by-row storage allocation of the form illustrated above.

As with simpler arrays, the name of the declared array defines a constant pointer which is the address of its first element. We could apply arithmetic in various ways to this pointer to reference array elements, bearing in mind the order of memory allocation defined, but if we declare an array as a two-dimensional structure we are more likely to want to access it in this way, by applying two indexes; for example:

a[2][3] = 0

would assign the value 0 to element number 3 in row number 2 of the array. Keep in mind that, as with simple arrays, dimensions are numbered from 0, so the array a has 'rows' numbered 0, 1 and 2, and columns numbered 0, 1, 2, 3 and 4. When referring to an array element in this way, the first subscript specifies the row-number, and the second the column-number.

It is possible to initialize a two-dimensional array when it is declared, thus:

```
int a[3][5] = {1,2,3,4,5,6,7,8,9,10,11,12,13,14,15};
```

or, for clarity, we can separate the rows with the use of additional curly brackets:

```
int a[3][5] = {
                {1,2,3,4,5},
                {6,7,8,9,10},
                {11,12,13,14,15}
              };
```

Everything we have said about two-dimensional arrays in C can be extended to arrays of three or more dimensions. A three-dimensional array can be thought of as an array of two-dimensional arrays, and declared thus:

```
int cube[3][2][4] = {
                      {{1,2,3,4},{5,6,7,8}},
                      {{9,10,11,12},{13,14,15,16}},
                      {{17,18,19,20},{21,22,23,24}}
                    };
```

Here, the layout used reflects our picture of **cube** as an array of three elements, each of which is an array of two rows and four columns. The order written also defines the storage order implied by the declaration. Likewise, a four-dimensional array can be conceived as an array of three-dimensional arrays and so on, indefinitely (although there is likely to be a system-dependent limit on the number of dimensions allowable).

Multi-dimensional array parameters

As the array name is simply a pointer, we can use it as the actual parameter for a function call to correspond to a formal parameter that is of the appropriate pointer type. This does not, however, enable us to access the array using row and column indexes unless further information is provided. In

the case of a two-dimensional array, the minimum information which must
be provided to define the structure of the array is the size of the *second*
dimension, i.e. the size of each 'row'.

Consider the function defined in Figure 3.20. The first formal parameter
of this function specifies a two-dimensional array, the size of whose second
dimension is defined. This is sufficient to enable a reference such as:

`table[i][j]`

within the function body to be translated correctly by the compiler. It is
permissible to make the size of the first dimension explicit also, although
this is not necessary.

```
/* Illustrates the use of a 2D array as a parameter
 * to a function. Function sets up a table so that
 * element table[i][j] contains i to the power j. */

void setup_powers(int table[][MAX_POWER+1], int max_base)
{
    int i,j,next_power;

    for (i=0;i<max_base;i++)
    {
        for (j=0,next_power=1; j<=MAX_POWER;j++)
        {
            table[i][j]=next_power;
            next_power=next_power*i;
        }
    }
    table[0][0]=0; /* special case */
}
```

Figure 3.20   A function with a 2D array parameter

As in other cases, dimensions, when included, must be constant expressions. This highlights the weakness of this method, as the dimensions must
therefore be bound at compile time into the code for the function, limiting
its generality. In the example used, this has been relaxed somewhat by
passing the size of the first dimension as a separate parameter, which need
not be a constant, although the row-size of the array remains fixed.

To escape this limitation, we must revert to the use of pointer-type parameters. In the program of Figure 3.21, the function `setup_powers()` has been rewritten so that its array parameter `table` is now defined to be of type `int *` rather than as an explicit two-dimensional array. (In fact, of course, the value passed as the actual parameter will in each case be the address of the array.) Within the function, it is no longer possible to index the parameter explicitly, but equivalent effects are achieved by passing the row and column sizes as (variable) parameters, to define the limits of the array. Within the loop that assigns the powers, the array is treated as a simple linear structure, the pointer to which is incremented on each loop traversal. This example underlines the need to be aware of the way in which the array is physically organized in the memory; higher-level languages than C can hide this from us because they do not usually offer the freedom to manipulate pointers which is available in C.

In Figure 3.21, the function is used in a complete program which also illustrates the use of `malloc()` and `free()`. The overall effect is that the size of the table of powers to be printed is determined at run-time, from data supplied by the user. The program uses `malloc()` to allocate sufficient space to store the table, and then invokes the functions `setup_powers()` and `print_matrix()` to calculate and print the values. The actual parameter `table_ptr` to each of these functions, which defines the address of the array, is the pointer-value returned as the result of the call of `malloc()`.

Other array forms

The freedom that C offers in the manipulation of pointers also allows us to organize array forms with, for example, variable row lengths. Figure 3.22 illustrates this capability. In this program a table of `float` values is set up, each of which represents a single reading obtained in the course of a particular scientific experiment. Each experiment has a different number of readings, however, so the structure created may be visualized as something like this:

```
#include <stdio.h>
#include <stdlib.h>

/* Illustrates the use of 2D arrays as a parameter
 * to a function accessed via pointers.
 * Using ptrs allows the function to set up any size arrays.
 * Function sets up a table so that element table[i][j]
 * contains i to the power j. */
void setup_powers(int *table,int num_rows,int num_cols)
{
    int i,j,next_power, *table_start = table;

    for (i=0;i<num_rows;i++)
    {
        for (j=0,next_power=1; j<num_cols;j++,table++)
        {
            *table=next_power;
            next_power=next_power*i;
        }
    }
    *table_start=0; /* special case */
}

/*------------------------------------------------------------*/

/* A function to print out a 2D array in tabular form. */
void print_matrix(int *matrix,int num_rows,int num_cols)
{
    int i,j;

    for (i=0;i<num_rows;i++)
    {
        for (j=0;j<num_cols;j++,matrix++)
        {
            printf("%d ",*matrix);
        }
        printf("\n");
    }
}

/*------------------------------------------------------------*/
```

```
/* A program to set up and print out a table of powers.
 * The program prompts for the table size and uses malloc()
 * to obtain space for the table. */
main()
{
    int max_power,max_base, *table_ptr;

    printf("What's the highest base you want to use?");
    scanf("%d",&max_base);

    printf("What's the biggest power you want to raise to?");
    scanf("%d",&max_power);

    table_ptr=malloc(sizeof(int)*(max_power+1)*(max_base+1));

    if (table_ptr==NULL)
    {
        printf("malloc could not meet request");
        exit(1);
    }

    setup_powers(table_ptr,max_base+1,max_power+1);
    print_matrix(table_ptr,max_base+1,max_power+1);
    free(table_ptr);
}
```

Figure 3.21   Using pointers to reference a 2D array parameter

To create this structure within the program, the `main()` function of
Figure 3.22 first invokes `malloc()` to obtain space for an array of pointers.
Notice the form of the declaration used:

`float **results;`

declares 'a pointer to a pointer to a **float**'. The program uses the variable
results to contain the address of an array, the elements of which will be
the addresses of arrays of **float** type.

The actual arrays to contain the readings are created within the function
`input_results()`. For each experiment in turn, the function obtains as
input the number of readings expected. The assignment:

```
#include <stdio.h>
#include <stdlib.h>

/*
 * This program illustrates how 'funny' shaped arrays can be
 * set up. Here we want to record the reading from a number
 * of experiments. The experiments have a different number
 * of readings.
 */

void input_results(int, int *, float **);

main()
{
   float **results;
   int *num_results;
   int experiments;

   printf("How many experiments took place? ");
   scanf("%d",&experiments);

   num_results = malloc(sizeof(int)*experiments);
   results = malloc(sizeof(float *)*experiments);

   if (num_results==NULL || results==NULL)
   {
      printf("not enough memory left - sorry\n");
      exit(1);
   }

   input_results(experiments,num_results,results);

   /*
    * presumably we would go on to use the results
    */
}
/*----------------------------------------------------------*/
```

```
/*
 * 'num_experiments' holds the number of experiments.
 * 'num_readings' is an integer array with 'num_experiments'
 * elements. Each element gives the number of readings for
 * that experiment. 'readings' is an array of pointers to
 * floats. Thus representing a two-dimensional array with
 * variable size rows.
 */

void input_results(int num_experiments,int *num_readings,
                                         float **readings)
{
    int i,j,num; float *ptr;

    for (i=0;i<num_experiments;i++)
    {
        printf("Number of readings for experiment %d? ",i);
        scanf("%d",&num);
        *num_readings++ = num;
        ptr = malloc(sizeof(float)*num);
        if (ptr == NULL)
        {
            printf("not enough memory left - sorry\n");
            exit(1);
        }
        *readings++ = ptr;
        printf("input the %d readings for experiment %d\n",
                                                     num,i);
        for (j=0;j<num;j++,ptr++) scanf("%f",ptr);
    }
}
```

Figure 3.22   An example of an array with varying row sizes

*num_readings++ = num

assigns this number to an element of the array `num_results` which is passed
as the actual parameter corresponding to `num_readings`, and increments
the pointer to this array each time the loop is traversed; notice again the
use of the pointer parameter to obtain a reference to the array which is the
actual parameter.

The function goes on to create, through `malloc()`, an array of size `num`
elements of type `float`, which will be used to contain the set of readings
for a single experiment. The pointer to this array is assigned to an element
of the pointer array `results`, using the assignment:

```
*readings++ = ptr; /* the actual parameter corresponding to
                       'readings' is 'results' */
```

Notice that the type of the formal parameter `readings` is 'pointer to
pointer to `float`'; i.e. the value passed as the actual parameter will be the
address of an array (`results`) the elements of which are themselves array
addresses.

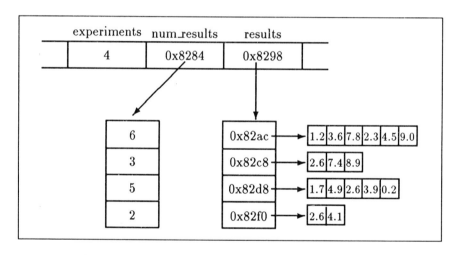

Figure 3.23   Memory layout for variable-sized arrays

For a set of four experiments, the data structures created might look
something like the illustration in Figure 3.23. Here we see that the array
`num_results` (stored, notionally, in four consecutive locations starting at
address 0x8284) contains the values of `num_readings` obtained for each of
the four experiments. The variable `results` contains a pointer (address

0x8298) to an array of pointers, each of which is the address of a different array of values set up by a separate call of `malloc()`. With these values, the command:

> *? show *results*

to our debugging system would produce the response:

> *0x8298   0x82ac*

while the command:

> *? show **results*

would display:

> *0x82ac   1.2*

3.5   Static and register variables

In Chapter 2, we introduced the concept of a variable's **storage class**, a property which defines its **scope** and its **lifetime**. The storage class **extern** describes a global variable, whose scope is the entire program text, and whose lifetime is the duration of the program's execution. The storage class **auto** represents a local variable, whose scope is confined to the function within which it is declared, and whose lifetime is a single invocation (call) of that function.

This is now a convenient point to describe the two remaining storage classes that were introduced in Chapter 2; **static** and **register** variables.

Static variables

When a local variable is declared to be of **static** storage class, its scope remains restricted to the function within which it is declared, but its lifetime becomes the duration of the program's execution; hence, its value (unlike normal local variables of **auto** class) is preserved between calls of the function. The program of Figure 3.24 illustrates a simple application.

Here, each call of the function **next_factorial()** returns the next in the sequence of factorial values. To enable it to do this, the function retains in static variables the value of the previous factorial calculated (**last_fact**)

```
/* This program illustrates the use of static internal
 * variables. Note how the initialization only applies
 * the first time the function is called. */
#include <stdio.h>

int next_factorial(void)
{
    static int n=0,last_fact=1;

    n++;
    last_fact = last_fact*n;
    return last_fact;
}

/*--------------------------------------------------------------*/

main()
{
    int i;

    for(i=1; i<=10; i++)
        printf("factorial %-d = %-d\n",i,next_factorial() );
}
```

Figure 3.24   Example of a static internal variable

and the value of n, used to calculate this, that is incremented on each call
of the function. Note the form of declaration used:

```
static int n=0,last_fact=1;
```

The *initialization* of a static variable (n=0,last_fact=1, in this case) is
performed only once, when the function is first invoked. Subsequent calls
of the function will use the values of these variables preserved from earlier
calls.

When the prefix static is applied to a **global** variable declaration, its
significance is rather different. Again, the lifetime of the variable is the
duration of the program's execution, but now the scope of the variable is
restricted to the *file* within which the declaration occurs.

Suppose, for example, we wish to define two functions, each of which manipulates a common variable **counts** (Figure 3.25). Because the variable is used by both functions, it is necessary to declare it externally. However, it might not be necessary for any other function to use this variable, and in this case it would be desirable to 'hide' the variable to prevent invalid references to it, and to avoid problems of name-clashes with other function variables.

```
static int count=0;

arrive(void)
{
    count++;
}

/*--------------------------------------------------------------*/

depart(void)
{
    count--;
}
```

Figure 3.25   Example of a static external variable

The solution is to define **counts** to be a static variable, and to contain its declaration and that of the two functions which use it within a separate file. (In Chapter 5 we go on to explain how a program stored in a number of separate files is managed.) The effect of this is to create a **package** containing the two functions, within which the global variable **counts** is hidden; i.e. its name is inaccessible to the rest of the program.

Register variables

The prefix **register** to the declaration of a local variable in C indicates to the compiler that we wish this variable, if possible, to be contained within a machine register rather than a main memory location. Thus the declaration:

> **register int i;**

will declare a variable **i**, of type **int**, whose storage class is **register**.

```
/* This program illustrates how register variables
 * can be used to make programs more time-efficient. */

#include <stdio.h>
#define MAX_SIZE 10000

/* Function to perform dot product */

double dot(register double *x,register double *y,
                                      register int n)
{
   double sum=0;

   for ( ;n-- >0; )
      sum = sum + (*x++) * (*y++) ;

   return sum;
}

/*----------------------------------------------------------*/

double a[MAX_SIZE];
double b[MAX_SIZE];

main()
{
   int i;

   for (i=0; i<MAX_SIZE; i++)
   {
      a[i]=i;
      b[i]=1;
   }

   /* most of the time will be spent here */
   for (i=0; i<200; i++)
      dot(a,b,MAX_SIZE);

   printf("dot product = %f\n",dot(a,b,MAX_SIZE));
}
```

Figure 3.26   Example of the use of register variables - dot()

We can apply this kind of declaration only to local variables, including formal parameters of functions. There are also likely to be machine-dependent restrictions on the number of register variables that can be within scope at any one time, and possibly on the types that can be declared for register variables. However, if the compiler is unable to allocate a machine register for a variable declared in this way, it will implement the declaration by allocating a memory location, i.e. treating the declaration as if the prefix **register** were not used.

In most respects, register variables behave like other local variables, although we cannot apply the **&** operator to obtain the address of a register variable. We expect, however, that the use of this storage class will result in a faster (and perhaps more compact) program implementation. Register variables are thus used principally to contain values which have a very high rate of access in the program, such as loop counters and array indices, and from which a more efficient implementation will yield worthwhile performance gains. It is possible, however, that a modern optimizing compiler will achieve as good or better results unaided, so it might be argued that **register** variables are an obsolescent remnant of C's origins as a low-level systems programming language.

The program of Figure 3.26 uses register variables to contain the formal parameters of the function dot(). These parameters include an integer n that defines the size of two arrays. The function uses n as a counter for a loop in which corresponding elements of the two arrays are multiplied together and added to a running total. Each traversal of the loop requires at least one reference to the variable n, and also to each of the parameters x and y which point to the two arrays; in fact, depending on the machine-level implementation of the loop, there are likely to be two or more references to each of the locations concerned. Declaring the formal parameters to be **register** variables enables the compiler to make use of machine registers to aid efficient implementation of this tight loop.

If the machine you are using enables you to time the execution of a program, you may find it interesting to compare the execution time of the program of Figure 3.26 with the time taken to perform the program when the function parameters are declared without the prefix **register**. Usually, of course, we would think about the use of register variables only as a final optimization of a program once it has been written and tested.

3.6 Exercises

1. Write a function that takes two strings as arguments and indicates if the first string is a substring of the second.

2. Write a function to reverse the order of the sequence of characters in a string.

3. The publicity department of a holiday camp wish to determine the success of their new advertising campaign launched at the start of the year by comparing the number of visitors this year with last. Write a program that takes as input, firstly, the monthly visitors figures for last year, and secondly, the monthly visitors figures for the current year. The program should then print out a vertical histogram showing the *difference* in the number of visitors for each month this year compared to last.

4. Write a function to sort a set of reals into ascending order.

5. Write a function which indicates if a real number lies within a given numeric range. If it does, the function should also give the amount by which this real number is greater than the base of the numeric range.

6. Consider the following picture:

Storing files which contain simple textual pictures like the one above can be wasteful in terms of filestore. A more efficient way to store the contents of such a file would be as a sequence of numbers which 'compress' the textual information. Whenever we wish to display the picture we can generate it from the number sequence.

Write a program to read in a picture and compress it according to the following:

(a) Pictures are composed of only two characters, a foreground character and a background character.

(b) The compressed form of a picture is a sequence of integers representing the number of consecutive characters to be printed of the foreground and background characters *alternately*.

(c) Thus, the sequence:

2 4 1 1 1 4 2

is the compressed form of

##....#.#....##

Your program should read in the height (number of lines) and width (number of characters on a line) of the picture.

Write a second program to generate a picture from its compressed form, again first inputting the height and width of the picture. Begin by writing a function which can be used to print out a given character a given number of times; the function should also be given the maximum line length for printing. The function will need to remember how many character positions are available for printing on the current line.

Note: As file-handling within C is not covered until Chapter 5, in order to test both these programs we assume that the input data is stored in a file from which the input stream to the executable program can be redirected. (The output from both programs should similarly be redirected to files.)

7. Write a function that will deliver a unique name each time it is called.

8. Write a program that will eliminate all duplicates from a list of integer values. All values input should be in the range 1 to N, where N is input at the start of the program. Any input values not in this range should be ignored. The list will be terminated by -1.

9. Write a function which takes as arguments two zero-terminated integer arrays and returns a third zero-terminated integer array which is composed of the non-zero elements of the two arrays concatenated together.

10. A 'magic square' is a square matrix $n \times n$ in which all integers in the range 1 to n^2 occur only once and all rows, columns and diagonals add up to the same value. Write a function that will determine whether or not a given matrix is a magic square.

11. The 'Game of Life' was invented by a mathematician who intended it should simulate the evolution of an idealized colony of bacteria. In this game, a bacteria colony lives in a grid of cells in which each germ occupies its own cell somewhere on the grid. Every so often the colony undergoes a life-cycle which produces the next generation of bacteria.

The survival of a germ during a life-cycle is determined by the number of its neighbouring cells which are also occupied (every cell has at most eight neighbours). The changes resulting from the life-cycle are as follows:

(a) If a germ in a given cell has only one neighbour it will die through loneliness.

(b) If a germ has four or more neighbours it will die through overcrowding.

(c) If an empty cell has exactly three adjacent cells which are occupied, then a new germ will be born there.

All these changes take place simultaneously and the cells around the edge of the grid will always remain unoccupied.

Write a program that reads in the starting state of a colony of bacteria, using a 15 × 15 grid. The program should then simulate the evolution of the colony over a given number of life-cycles. Your program should print out the state of the colony after each life-cycle.

Try your program using the following as the starting colony (* indicates an occupied cell):

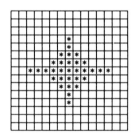

12. Data recording the toxicity level of a region of an ocean is held in a 3D array. There are 10 points on the east-west axis, 20 points on the north-south axis, and 15 depth points. Write a function which returns the average toxicity level surrounding a specified non-perimeter point. This is computed by averaging the toxicity levels of the 26 immediately neighbouring points.

13. Write a function to allocate memory for a triangular array of a given size. Write two further functions:

(a) to set the element i,j of the array;

(b) to return the contents of element i,j of the array.

14. Write a program which takes a list of words, passed as command-line arguments, and determines all the alphabetic characters common to every word in the list.

Chapter 4

Program sequence and control

4.1 Statements

Many of the ideas and program forms used in C to define the program sequence of execution were introduced in Chapter 2, and have been used subsequently in the examples of programs given. In this chapter we collect together and review these constructs, and also introduce the further ways in which program control structures are described in C.

The principal unit of program execution in C, as in many other high-level languages, is the **statement**. A statement in C can, in fact, be any **expression** terminated by a semicolon, so that a sequence such as:

$$x+y;x*3;$$

is a perfectly valid pair of statements in C. Statements such as these perform a calculation the result of which is then discarded; thus they are not usually useful. More typically, the statement:

$$x++;$$

is an example of a simple expression-statement that *is* useful because, in addition to calculating a value, it also changes the value of the variable **x**.

Statements terminated by semicolons are normally executed in order, in the sequence written. A sequence of statements enclosed within curly brackets is a **compound statement**, or **block**; for example:

```
{ int a,b;

  printf("Input a and b");
  scanf("%d%d",&a,&b);
  printf("Average=%f\n",(a+b)/2.0);
}
```

The purpose of this is twofold. First, it is necessary to use these brackets to define the extent of program constructs such as a function body, or the body of a loop. Second, we can include declarations at the start of a compound statement (as we have in this example), and the **scope** of these declarations will be confined to the statements within the brackets; i.e. the declarations will be local to this compound statement. Notice that, in general, the closing bracket of a compound statement does *not* require to be followed by a terminating semicolon. However, when a semicolon does occur in isolation, it will usually be interpreted as a **null** statement, which has no effect in execution.

Assignment statements

The most frequently used type of **simple statement** is the assignment statement which, as we explained in Chapter 2, is another instance of a statement that is an expression. The effect of the statement:

```
a = b+3;
```

is to assign the value obtained by calculating b+3 to the variable a, and the same value will be the result of the expression. This interpretation derives from the definition of the symbol '=' as an **operator** that both produces a result and has an associated effect on its left-hand operand.

C has a number of other assignment operators which perform commonly-used kinds of assignment. For example:

```
total += next*3;
```

uses the special assignment operator '+=' to add the value of the expression next*3 *into* total; i.e. the effect is the same as:

```
total = total+next*3;
```

The operator += (which we can read as 'plus and becomes equal to') is not only a useful shorthand notation for a very common operation, but is also likely to be implemented more efficiently in the object program. There exist assignment operators of this kind corresponding to most of the diadic operators of C; i.e.:

```
+ - * / % & | ^ << >>
```

all have corresponding assignment operators. For example:

```
signal &= mask; /* 'AND' the mask bits into signal */
```

In each case, the value of the assignment-expression is again the value which is assigned finally to the left-hand operand; this is relevant in statements such as:

```
a=b+=2; /* add 2 to b; assign the result to b and to a */
```

Operator precedence

Now that we have introduced nearly all of the operators used in C, this is an appropriate point to define the full table of operator precedence (Figure 4.1).

highest	()	[]	->	.						
	!	~	++	--	+	-	*	&	(cast)	sizeof
	*	/	%							
	+	-								
	<<	>>								
	<	<=	>	>=						
	==	!=								
	&									
	^									
	|									
	&&									
	||									
	?:									
	=	+=	-=	*=	/=	%=	&=	^=	|=	<<= >>=
lowest	,									

Figure 4.1   Table of operator precedences

Note that the brackets () used when a function call is made, and the brackets [] used to enclose array subscripts, are treated as high-priority operators applied, respectively, to the function name and the array identifier (or pointer). The next highest set of operators are the monadic (unary) operators, amongst which are included the type coercion or **cast** operations

The diadic operators have lower priorities, and the assignment operators lowest of all (apart from the 'comma' operator that separates a sequence of expressions).

Three operators in this table have not yet been described. The ternary condition operator ?: will be introduced in the next section, and -> and . in Chapter 6 when we discuss **structures**.

4.2 Conditional statements

The form of conditional statement introduced in Chapter 2 is written either:

$$\text{if } (< condition >)$$
$$< statement >;$$

or:

$$\text{if } (< condition >)$$
$$< statement1 >;$$
$$\text{else}$$
$$< statement2 >;$$

Note that any of the subsidiary statements included within a conditional statement can be compound statements, enclosed within curly brackets, which may also include local declarations.

A more concise notation, sometimes used, employs the *ternary* **condition operator** ?:. This operator forms an expression with three operands, thus:

$$< condition > ? < expression1 > : < expression2 >$$

The question-mark and the colon are regarded as being two parts of the same ternary operator. The result of this ternary expression is the value of $< expression1 >$ if the $< condition >$ is true, or otherwise the value of $< expression2 >$. For example, the statement:

```
largest = a>b ? a : b;
```

assigns to `largest` the value of `a` (if a>b) or the value of `b`, otherwise. In this example (as is usually the case when the condition operator is employed) we are using it to form a conditional *expression* rather than a conditional statement (for which the `if...else` form is more appropriate). Another example:

```
printf("%s Smith\n",sex=='m' ? "Mr" : "Mrs");
```

will print either "**Mr Smith**" or "**Mrs Smith**", depending on the value of the variable **sex**.

Nesting of 'if' statements

It is permissible to 'nest' one **if** statement within another, thus:

```
if (< condition1 >)
  if (< condition2 >)
    < statement1 >;
  else
    < statement2 >;
```

In this case, the rule is that **else** associates with the most recently preceding unattached **if** (i.e. nesting is from the 'inside' of the nested structure towards the 'outside'). In the example above, the < *statement2* > following **else** is part of the second, or 'inner' **if** statement. Similarly, in the following example:

```
if (next>largest_so_far || next<smallest_so_far)
  if (next>largest_so_far) largest_so_far=next;
  else smallest_so_far=next;
```

It is also possible to chain **if** statements in sequence to produce a 'multi-way' conditional statement, thus:

```
if (< condition1 >)
  < statement1 >;
else if (< condition2 >)
  < statement2 >;
else if (< condition3 >)
  < statement3 >;
        .
        .
        .
else if (< conditionN >)
  < statementN >;
```

e.g.

```
if (mark>=70)
    printf("Well done, grade A\n");
else if (mark>=60)
    printf("Quite good, grade B\n");
else if (mark>=50)
    printf("Ok, grade C\n");
else printf("Whoops! fail\n");
```

Switch statements

A different form of multiway conditional statement is provided by the **switch** statement. This takes the form:

```
switch (< switch value >)
{
  case < value1 >:
  < statement list1 >
  case < value2 >:
  < statement list2 >
  case < value3 >:
    < statement list3 >

        .

        .

        .

  case < valueN >:
  < statement listN >
  default: < statement list default >
}
```

In this construction, the < *switch value* > must be an integer-valued expression, which is first evaluated. This value is then compared with the set of values < *value1* >, < *value2* >...that identify the different cases; each of these must be a **constant** expression, and each should have a different value. If the switch-value is successfully matched with one of these constant case-values, then control transfers to the sequence of statements associated with that case. If no match is found, then control passes to the default-list statements. The **default** part of the switch is optional; if it is omitted, the effect is that no statements are performed unless a match of the switch-value is found. It is also possible to omit the list of statements associated with any particular case-value; the effect of this is that two (or more) case-values will be associated with the same statement list.

Provided that each case-value is different, the order in which they are written (including the **default** case) is not significant. If two case-values are the same, then the first match encountered will be selected.

Figure 4.2 illustrates the use of a switch statement. In this program, a single character (**base**) is used to define the number-base of a binary, octal or decimal number that is read as a sequence of characters. This character is used to select the appropriate case used in the number-construction loop. Recall that a **char** in C is a particular type of integer, so 'b', 'B', etc. are integer-valued constants. Notice also the use of both 'b' and 'B' (and also 'o' and 'O') to 'label' the same sequence of statements; i.e. the two cases are merged.

```c
/* The function 'input_num()' reads in a number from the
 * standard input channel. The first character indicates
 * how to interpret the rest of the number. B or b for
 * binary, O or o for octal and D or d for decimal. */
#include <stdio.h>
#define TRUE 1
#define FALSE 0

int input_num(void)
{
   char base,digit;
   int not_end,number;

   printf("Input a binary, octal, or decimal number\n");
   scanf("%c",&base);

   for (not_end=TRUE,number=0;not_end; )
   {
      scanf("%c",&digit);

      switch(base)
      {
         case 'b':
         case 'B': if (digit>='0' && digit<='1')
                      number = number*2 + digit-'0';
                   else not_end=FALSE;
                   break;
         case 'o':
         case 'O': if (digit>='0' && digit<='7')
                      number = number*8 + digit-'0';
                   else not_end=FALSE;
                   break;
         case 'd': if (digit>='0' && digit<='9')
                      number = number*10 + digit-'0';
                   else not_end=FALSE;
                   break;
         default: printf("error-base indicator missing\n");
                  not_end=FALSE;
      }
   }
   return number;
}
```

```
/*-----------------------------------------------------------*/

main()
{
    printf("number input=%d\n",input_num());
}
```

Figure 4.2   Example of a **switch** statement

Figure 4.2 also includes a statement we have not previously described. The statement:

break;

when executed within a switch statement, causes termination of the switch; i.e. an exit is made to the end of the switch statement. It is necessary, in this example, and indeed in most cases within switch statements, because selection of a case within a switch statement causes a simple **transfer of control** to the corresponding case-statements. Once these have been executed, execution continues on to the *next* sequence of statements unless a **break** (or other change of control) intervenes. Thus, in Figure 4.2, selection and execution of the **if** statement associated with case '**B**' would be immediately followed by execution of the following **if** statement associated with case '**o**'. The interposition of the **break** statement at the end of the first case ensures that, after the statement associated with case '**B**' has been executed, control passes out of the switch statement and execution proceeds with the statement following (in this case, the end of the loop).

A **break** statement is legal in only two contexts: either, as in this example, within a switch statement, or within a loop. In the latter case, the effect is similar, i.e. execution of the **break** statement results in immediate termination of the loop.

4.3 Loops

We have so far described only one kind of loop: this is the **for** statement, which was introduced in Chapter 2. C also has two other forms of loop: the **while** statement and the **do-while** statement. Recall that the general form of a **for** statement is:

for (< *initialization section* >;< *condition section* >;< *end section* >)
< *statement* >;

This form is particularly suitable for expressing the kind of loop in which some variable (the **control** variable) is first initialized, is amended at the end of each traversal of the loop, and is used to control termination of the loop. For example:

```
for (sum=0,i=0; i<limit; i++)
    sum += data[i];
```

The **for** statement defines a very general loop construction, which (as we have seen in some earlier examples) can be used to express a very wide variety of kinds of loop. Some of these can be expressed more clearly and simply using the **while** statement, which has the general form:

while (< *condition* >)
< *statement* >;

In this kind of loop the < *statement* > is repeated as long as the < *condition* > remains true. The condition is tested at the start of each cycle of the loop; if it is false at the commencement of the loop, the body of the loop will not be executed at all.

The use of the **while** loop is illustrated in Figure 4.3. Notice that the < *condition* > defined in this loop is the expression (*str++) which increments the string pointer **str** at the start of each cycle of the loop. The *value* of this expression is the value obtained from the location pointed to by **str**; as long as this value is non-zero, the condition being tested will be TRUE. Thus, the effect is that the loop terminates when the zero-valued string terminating character is found.

The **do-while** loop is quite similar, but in this case the terminating condition is tested at the *end* of each cycle of the loop, rather than the beginning:

do
< *statement* >;
while (< *condition* >)

The implication is that the < *statement* > will be performed at least once, and its execution will be repeated as long as the condition remains true. Figure 4.4 shows its application in a function that simulates the repeated throwing of a die until a particular value is obtained. In this function a second function **throw_die()** is invoked to generate the simulated value of the die. This function in turn calls a standard library function, **rand()**.

that returns a pseudo-random number in the range 0 to **RAND_MAX**, which is a system-dependent constant whose value is at least 32767.

```c
#include <stdio.h>
/*
 * This function illustrates the use of a 'while' loop.
 * 'string_length' returns the length of the string which
 * is pointed at by its argument 'str'
 */
int string_length(char *str)
{
    int length=0;
    while (*str++)
        length++;

    return length;
}

/*----------------------------------------------------------*/

char test_data[]="A 21 character string";

main()
{
    printf("string '%s' contains %d characters\n",
                    test_data,string_length(test_data));
}
```

Figure 4.3   Example of the use of a **while** loop

Notice that, in this example, the function **throw_die()** has been used *before* its declaration, even though no function prototype has been used to specify it. This is possible because, in these cases, the C compiler assumes that the undeclared function has a result of type **int**. In the case of **throw_die()**, this assumption is correct and, as the function has no parameters, the compiler has no difficulty in making the function call correctly.

While in many contexts the inclusion of a redundant semicolon in the program sequence is interpreted, harmlessly, as a null statement, particular care is needed with the form of loop constructions. Consider, for example, the sequence:

```
/*This function illustrates the use of a 'do-while' loop.
 * The function 'throw_to_get' simulates the throwing of a
 * die until the die shows the argument 'number'. */
#include <stdio.h>
#include <stdlib.h>

int throw_to_get(int number)
{
    int count=0,next;
    do
    {
        next=throw_die();
        count++;
    }
    while (next !=number);
    return count;
}

/*----------------------------------------------------------*/

/* 'throw_die' simulates the throwing of a die.
 * It uses the standard library routine rand() */

int throw_die(void)
{ return(rand()%6+1); }
```

Figure 4.4   Example of the use of a do-while loop

```
for (i=0;i<n;i++);
    a[i]=b[i];
```

This loop, intended to assign the elements of an array, does not in fact
have the desired effect. The reason is that the semicolon which follows
the closing bracket of the control section is interpreted as being the (null)
statement of the loop body. Thus the only assignment to take place will
follow completion of the loop, and will assign a[n]=b[n].

Other changes of control

In general, it is good programming practice to avoid arbitrary changes of control (jumps) in the program sequence; with some thought it is usually possible to achieve the effects we want using well-structured conditional statements and loop forms. Sometimes, however, it is useful to be able to make a premature exit from a loop or other program structure, and we have already seen in the case of the **switch** statement the necessity to define a way of transferring control to the end of the statement when the required case has been dealt with.

C provides a number of ways of achieving these changes of control, each with slightly different characteristics. The most general is the **goto** statement, which transfers control to a labelled statement:

$$< label >: \qquad .$$
$$.$$
$$.$$
$$.$$
$$\textbf{goto} < label >;$$

A label is an identifier formed using the same rules as apply to the formation of variable names. Any statement may be labelled by prefixing it with a label followed by a colon. A change in control (jump) to this statement can then be effected by a **goto** statement occurring at any point within the same function.

We will not rehearse all the arguments against the indiscriminate use of the **goto** statement. It will be sufficient to say that there are, infrequently, cases where its use *is* appropriate; for example, when it is necessary to terminate the execution of a deeply nested sequence of loops (Figure 4.5).

Three other ways of termination are available for dropping out of loops and other program structures: the **break** statement, the **continue** statement, and the **exit()** function.

The **break** statement, as we have already seen, provides a means of terminating a **switch** statement, transferring control to the statement following the switch. When used within a loop (of any type) its effect is to terminate the loop's execution, transferring control to the statement following the loop (or, in the case of an inner loop, to the next enclosing loop).

The **continue** statement can be used only within a loop. Its effect is to terminate the current cycle of the loop, passing control to the point in the loop construction at which the terminating condition is tested. For a **while** or **do-while** loop, this is the < *condition* > defined, and for a **for** loop, it is the start of the < *end section* > of the loop.

```
for (i=0; i<n; i++)
{
    for (j=0; j<m; j++)
    {
        for (k=0; k<p; k++)
        {
            scanf("%d",&data[i][j][k]);
            if (data[i][j][k]<0) goto error_exit
        }
    }
}
.

.

.

error_exit: printf("data error\n");
```

Figure 4.5   Jumping out of nested loops

The **exit()** function terminates execution of the program at the point at which it is invoked. The function takes a parameter of type **int**, that may be used to pass a value defining the terminating condition to the calling environment of the program.

Finally, a reminder about the **return** statement, execution of which brings about immediate termination of the function within which it occurs. The statement takes the form:

return < *expression* >;

where the < *expression* > is optional and, if included, defines the value that is returned as the result of the function call.

4.4   Exercises

1. Implement a program to mimic a simple desk calculator that has an accumulator and a single memory. Your program should:

   (a) Accept real numbers as numeric data.

   (b) Respond to the following characters as indicated:

       C   clear accumulator

+   add incoming numeric value to the accumulator

−   subtract incoming numeric value from accumulator

*   multiply the accumulator by the incoming numeric data value and store result in accumulator

/   divide the accumulator by the incoming numeric data value and store the result in the accumulator

=   display the accumulator

L   load the memory with the accumulator

M operator   perform the operation specified between the accumulator and the memory, placing result in the accumulator; (i.e. will be followed by one of +,−,*,/ operators). For example, M/ will divide accumulator by memory

Z   clear the memory

Q   end the program

(c) Your program should not distinguish between lower and upper case letters.

2. Write a function that prints out the value and suit of a playing card. The card is represented by a number in the range 0 to 51, passed as a parameter, where:

      0 to 12 represents hearts
      13 to 25 represents clubs
      26 to 38 represents diamonds
      39 to 51 represents spades

Use your function in a program to generate and print out a hand of cards for the game of bridge.

3. Write a program that randomly generates a 'secret' number and allows the user to guess its value. The program should respond to each guess input by indicating whether the secret number is higher or lower than the guess. The program terminates with a successful guess.

4. Write a program that plays the game of 'moo'. To play this game your program should generate three hidden values, each in the range 0 to 9, which the player is required to guess, in the correct order. A player inputs a guess in the form of three integer values, to which the program responds by indicating the accuracy of the guess as follows:

(a) A completely incorrect guess generates no response.

(b) If a value has been guessed correctly and is in the correct position, the program registers a **bull**.

(c) If a value has been guessed correctly but in the wrong position the program registers a **cow**.

For example, assuming the three hidden values are 5 9 2, then:

    a guess of 2 9 7 would generate the response: **1 bull and 1 cow**
    a guess of 9 2 5 would generate the response: **3 cows**

Thus, a guess of three bulls successfully terminates the game. The program should then display the number of guesses taken.

5. Write a function to generate a bingo card. The bingo card should:

   (a) have three rows;

   (b) have nine columns;

   (c) contain 15 different numbers in the range 1–90 (note: column entries do not have to be in ascending order);

   (d) have five numbers per row;

   (e) have its numbers placed in ascending order and placed in the appropriate column (1–9 in column 0, 10–19 in column 1, 20–29 in column 2, etc.).

6. Write a function that could be used to print out bingo cards generated by the above function.

   Simulate the playing of a game of bingo between 'n' people.

Chapter 5

Libraries and compilation

5.1   The compilation process

As we have already seen, many of the facilities of ANSI C are provided via
library functions such as `scanf()` and `malloc()`. These functions are
incorporated in standard libraries that should be provided as part of any
full ANSI C implementation. The C language environment also provides
for the use of locally-defined libraries of functions, and for other ways of
including in the program information that is not part of the immediate
program text.

This is achieved through a three-step compilation process, illustrated
in Figure 5.1. In the first stage, the source program is transcribed by a
preprocessor which performs two kinds of textual substitution: the inclusion of text taken from source files specified in `#include` directives, and
macro substitution corresponding to `#define` directives. The resulting C language program is then compiled in the usual way to produce an
object-program file. In the final stage, this file is linked with other object
files containing separately compiled functions, including standard library
functions, to produce an executable program.

Some aspects of this process are, naturally, system-dependent. What
is common to all implementations of ANSI C, however, is the facility for
separate compilation of C functions that can then be incorporated in an
executable program. In Chapter 1 we introduced an arbitrary command
for the compilation of a C program; for example:

$ ccompile firstprog.c welcome

was assumed to compile a C program contained in the file *firstprog.c*, to produce an executable program file with the name *welcome*. We also assumed, implicitly, that this executable program would include any library functions required by the program; in some systems, it may be necessary to specify this in the form of explicit parameters to the compilation command.

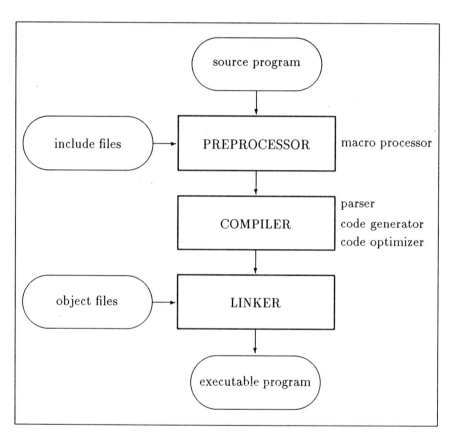

Figure 5.1   The C compilation sequence

More generally, if we wish to allow for the inclusion of separately compiled functions, it is necessary to separate the stages of the compilation process. We will assume that the command:

$ *ccomp someprog.c*

has the effect of compiling the program contained in the file *someprog.c* (including any necessary preprocessing) to produce an object program contained in the file *someprog.o.* The further command:

$ *link someprog.o somefunc.o mylib*

links this object program with another object program file, *somefunc.o* (which might contain a separately compiled function), and with functions taken from the library file, *mylib.* (We assume that any **standard** library files are linked automatically.) An executable program file is created, with the name *someprog.ex.*

The library file, *mylib,* might contain the object code for a number of separately compiled functions. The format of this kind of file is again, of course, system-dependent, but we will assume that a file of the appropriate type can be created by a command such as:

$ *archive mylib func1.o func2.o func3.o*

which creates a library file, namely *mylib,* incorporating the three named object files.

Most C environments should provide commands similar to these; in particular, those we have described are simplified versions of the commands **cc** (compile), **ld** (link) and **ar** (archive) available in most UNIX systems. They are sufficient to allow us to compile C functions independently, to include sets of functions in user-created libraries, and to use separately compiled functions and library routines in our programs.

5.2   The preprocessor

Source file inclusion

Directives to the C preprocessor are prefixed with the character **#**, which must occur as the first character of a line of the program text. The directive:

```
#include
```

is used to specify that text contained in a separate file is to be included in the source program at this point. Two forms of the directive may be used, corresponding in general to the substitution of user files and standard system files. In the form we have seen so far, a directive such as:

```
#include <stdio.h>
```

is used to specify the inclusion of text contained in a system file, *stdio.h*, which will be found in some system-defined way (for example, within some specific directory of files). The alternative form:

    #include "mydefs.h"

allows for the substitution of text contained in a normal 'user' file, in this case *mydefs.h*.

In earlier examples, we have used the first form of the directive in association with the use of library functions such as the standard input and output functions, *stdio*. Notice, however, that the line:

    #include <stdio.h>

does not itself bring about inclusion of the library functions in the object program; the **#include** directive is an instruction to the **preprocessor**, whereas the incorporation of library functions is, as we have explained, performed by the **linker**. What the file *stdio.h* does include is a set of declarations and other information that is required by functions in the associated library. This kind of information is called a **header file**, and by convention, the filename is given the suffix '.h' to indicate this. Most libraries of functions require an associated header file to be included in programs that use them; this applies both to standard libraries and to user-defined libraries. The header file must be included before any call of a function in the library, i.e. usually at the start of the program file.

Macroprocessing

We have so far introduced the directive **#define** only briefly, as a way of defining a literal constant used in a program. More generally, **#define** provides a facility for C language **macro substitution**.

The simplest kind of macro is defined by a directive of the form:

    #define < macro name >< macro string >

For example:

    #define TRUE 1

Like **#include**, the **#define** directive must begin at the start of a new line in the program; it can be placed anywhere within the text of a program, between program statements, as well as at the start of the file. Its effect is to define a **textual** substitution < macro string > for the < macro name > introduced. The C preprocessor responds by replacing each subsequent appearance of < macro name > in the program text by the associated

< *macro string* >; thus, in the example, each occurrence of the macro-name **TRUE** is replaced by the character **1**.

The rules for forming macro-names are the same as those for other identifiers; however, it is a convention that macro-names are formed using at least some upper-case letters to distinguish them from genuine variable names, which conventionally use lower-case letters only. The macro-string defined can contain any character, and can be made to extend over more than one line by terminating lines with the backslash character, '\' (back-slash characters *within* the line are treated as part of the string).

Macro substitution takes place throughout the program, except within text strings inside string quotes, which are transcribed literally. This kind of simple macro definition has a number of uses: to define symbolic constants (as in the example above), and equivalences for variable names; to define alternative notations for program constructs; and even to define shorthand forms for commonly-used program sequences. Usually, macros are defined at the start of the program file, and often these definitions are included in a header file substituted using #include.

Figure 5.2 contains a number of typical instances of simple macros. Notice, in particular, the way that the definitions of **BEGIN** (for an opening curly bracket), **END** (for a semicolon, followed on the next line by a closing curly bracket) and **BOOL** (providing an alternative name for the type **short**) are used to describe an alternative lexical representation for the language, giving the program text an ALGOL-like appearance.

Macros with parameters

More complex macro substitution is possible using macros with parameters. The macro definition:

> #define < *macro name* >(< *parameter list* >) < *macro string* >

introduces a macro-name with an associated list of (formal) parameter names, separated by commas. The parameter list is enclosed in brackets and must *immediately* follow the macro-name without any intervening spaces. The parameter names are again formed in the same way as proper variable names, and it is implicit that occurrences of these formal parameters will be found within the associated macro-string. When the macro is used, it must be associated with a list of actual parameters that will be **textually** substituted, in the same order, for the formal parameters. The effect of an application of the macro is therefore that the macro-string is substituted, with every occurrence of a formal parameter name within the string being replaced by its corresponding actual parameter string.

```
/* This program illustrates the use of #define. */
#define MAX_SIZE 1024
#define TRUE 1
#define FALSE 0
#define NULL 0

#define BOOL short
#define INT32 int

#define BEGIN {
#define END ;\
          }

#include <stdio.h>
main()
BEGIN
   BOOL not_found = TRUE;
   INT32 i,next,address;
   for (i=0; not_found && i<MAX_SIZE; i++)
   BEGIN
      scanf("%d%d",&address,&next);
      if (next==NULL) not_found = FALSE
   END
   printf("NULL found at address %d\n",address)
END
```

Figure 5.2   Some typical examples of the use of `#define`

Figure 5.3 should help to make this clear. Here, the macro BETWEEN defines a conditional expression to test whether the value of the formal parameter a is greater than that of the formal parameter b and less than that of c. In the program that follows, the macro BETWEEN is used with *actual* parameters z,x and y. The effect is that the preprocessor elaborates the line:

$$\text{if } (\text{BETWEEN}(z,x,y))$$

using the macro-string defined for BETWEEN, with z replacing a, x replacing b, and y replacing c, to produce:

$$\text{if } (z>x \text{ \&\& } z<y \text{ ? } 1 : 0)$$

```
/*
 * This program illustrates macros with more than
 * one parameter.
 */
#include <stdio.h>
#define TRUE 1
#define FALSE 0

#define BETWEEN(a,b,c)  a>b && a<c ? TRUE : FALSE

#define SWAP(type,num1,num2) \
        {\
            type temp; \
            temp=num1;\
            num1=num2;\
            num2=temp;\
        }
main()
{
    float x,y,z;

    printf("Input two real numbers ");
    scanf("%f%f",&x,&y);

    if (x>y) SWAP(float,x,y);

    printf("input a number ");
    scanf("%f",&z);

    if (BETWEEN(z,x,y))
       printf("%f is between %f and %f\n",z,x,y);
    else printf("%f is not between %f and %f\n",z,x,y);
}
```

Figure 5.3 Examples of macros with several parameters

(Note that other macro-definitions have been used to substitute 1 and 0 for
`TRUE` and `FALSE`.)

The other parameterized macro, `SWAP`, is treated similarly. Here, the
macro defines a declaration of a variable `temp` whose type is supplied as the
first parameter of the macro. The effect of the macro is to exchange the
values of its two other actual parameters. In the instance of `SWAP` found
within this program, the `type` parameter is `float`, so the preprocessor at
this point in the program substitutes the sequence:

```
{ float temp; temp = x; x = y; y = temp; }
```

Macros with parameters are similar in many respects to functions with
parameters, and are often used for similar purposes. It is important to
be aware of the differences, however: whereas parameter substitution in
function calls is dynamic, macro substitution is **textual**. This means that
(as in the example of `SWAP`, above) some forms of parameterization can be
used that would not be possible using function calls. It also means that
the effects of using macros are sometimes unexpectedly different from those
that would be obtained using functions.

Figure 5.4 illustrates some possible pitfalls. Consider a possible execution of this program:

```
input a binary number 111,
number = 7
SQUARE of 5 = 11
Table of squares from 0 to 10
  2      0
  4      6
  6      20
  8      42
 10      72
 12     110
```

The macro `ISBINARY` has been used, correctly, to determine whether the
sequence '111' defines a binary number, and the program has printed the
decimal number 7 which corresponds to this. It is clear, however, that
something has gone wrong in the calculations of squares of numbers, using
the macro `SQUARE`.

In fact, nothing is wrong with the definition of `SQUARE`, but both instances of its use illustrate the need for care in distinguishing between the
effects of macros and those of function calls. In the first case, the substitution for `SQUARE(3+2)` is:

```
3+2*3+2
```

```
/* This program is intended to illustrate macros with
 * parameters and some of the pitfalls. */
#define TRUE 1
#define FALSE 0
#include <stdio.h>
main()
{
#define ISBINARY(num) num=='1' || num=='0' ? TRUE : FALSE

    int number=0;
    char c;
    printf("input a binary number");
    while (scanf("%c",&c),ISBINARY(c))
        number = number*2+c-'0';
    printf("number = %d\n",number);

/* Note macros must be used with care. */
#define SQUARE(x) x*x
    printf("SQUARE of 5 = %d\n",SQUARE(3+2));

    number=0;
    printf("Table of squares from 0 to 10\n");
    while (number<11)
        printf("%2d      %3d\n",number,SQUARE(number++));
}
```

Figure 5.4   Careless use of macros

which, of course, is evaluated (correctly!) to give the answer 11. The problem has arisen because the actual parameter substituted is the text sequence **3+2**, *not* the value 5 which would be the actual parameter in the case of a function call.

In the second case, textual substitution produces:

```
printf("%2d      %3d\n",number,number++*number++);
```

The problem here is twofold. First, the incrementation of number occurs not once (as would be the case in a function call) but *twice*, as a result of the double textual substitution of the actual parameter. Hence the 'squares' tabulated are actually the values of 0*1, then 2*3, 4*5, 6*7, 8*9 and 10*11.

```
main()
{
   float x,y,z;

   printf("Input two real numbers ");
   scanf("%f%f",&x,&y);

   if (x>y) { float temp; temp=x; x=y; y=temp; } ;

   printf("input a number ");
   scanf("%f",&z);

   if ( z>x && z<y ? 1  : 0  )
      printf("%f is between %f and %f\n",z,x,y);
   else printf("%f is not between %f and %f\n",z,x,y);
}
```

```
main()
{
   int number=0;
   char c;
   printf("input a binary number");
   while (scanf("%c",&c),c=='1' || c=='0' ? 1  : 0  )
      number = number*2+c-'0';
   printf("number = %d\n",number);



   printf("SQUARE of 5 = %d\n",3+2*3+2 );

   number=0;
   printf("Table of squares from 0 to 10\n");
   while (number<11)
      printf("%2d      %3d\n",number,number++*number++ );
}
```

Figure 5.5 Examples 5.3 and 5.4 after macro substitution

Second, because the calculation of the expression (with the associated double incrementation of **number**) takes place *before* the **printf()** function is invoked, the value printed for **number** is always its value following this calculation.

Sometimes problems such as these become obvious when the program text following macro substitution is examined, and many compilers allow this to be done. Figure 5.5 shows the programs of Figures 5.3 and 5.4 in their form following the preprocessor stage of compilation, after macro substitution has taken place (we have not shown in this listing the text substituted for **#include** directives, which would also be included at this stage). Note also that the preprocessor removes all comments from the program text.

Finally, a macro-definition remains in force until the end of program compilation, unless it is removed by a directive:

#undef < *macro name* >

which, like the other preprocessor directives, must be written at the start of a line.

The preprocessor # and ## operators

Normally, macro substitution is suspended during preprocessing of text strings, to allow any literal sequence of characters to be included within string quotes. If we require to define a macro substitution for a text string, however, we can achieve this effect using the preprocessor **#** operator, which can be applied to a formal parameter in a macro-definition. Its effect is to cause the substitution of the actual parameter to be enclosed within string quotes.

Figure 5.6(a) shows the definition of a macro with two formal parameters, **x** and **y**. Within the macro-string, the occurrences of these parameters are prefixed by the **#** operator, indicating that the actual parameters are to be enclosed within quotes when they are substituted. The result after preprocessing the program is shown in Figure 5.6(b).

The preprocessor **##** operator is used to specify concatenation of macro parameters with each other, or with adjacent text. The effect of appending **##** to a formal parameter within the macro-string is to cause any 'white space' between the parameter and adjacent text to be removed when parameter substitution takes place. Figure 5.7 illustrates the use of this operator to define composite names by macro substitution; the sequence:

x##_bill

```
/* This program illustrates the use of the # preprocessor
 * operator to convert a macro formal parameter to a string.
 */
#include <stdio.h>

#define collective(x,y) \
   printf("A " #y " of " #x "\n");
main()
{
   collective(sheep,flock);
   collective(geese,gaggle);
   collective(lions,pride);
}
```

(a) Original program

```
main()
{
   printf("A " "flock" " of " "sheep" "\n"); ;
   printf("A " "gaggle" " of " "geese" "\n"); ;
   printf("A " "pride" " of " "lions" "\n"); ;
}
```

(b) Program after preprocessing

Figure 5.6   Preprocessing of the # operator

when the formal parameter **x** is replaced by the actual parameter **jims**, becomes **jims_bill**. Note that the double semicolon which appears at the end of the preprocessed program will cause no problems, as a semicolon on its own is a valid (null) statement.

Conditional compilation

A final group of preprocessor directives allows us to define sections of program text that are included in the preprocessed program only in defined circumstances. The **#if** and **#else** directives are used to specify **conditional compilation** with the same kind of construction as is used when writing a conditional statement using **if** and **else**. The difference is, of

```
/* This program illustrates the use of the ## preprocessor
 * operator to merge tokens. */

#include <stdio.h>

#define init(x) \
    float x ## _bill = 0.0; \
    int   x ## _count = 0;

main()
{
    init(jims);
}
```

(a) Original program

```
main()
{
    float jims_bill = 0.0; int   jims_count = 0;  ;
}
```

(b) Program after preprocessing

Figure 5.7   Preprocessing of the ## operator

course, that the directives **#if** and **#else** are dealt with entirely in the preprocessing stage of compilation to define the final program text.

The directive:

#if < *condition* >

causes the specified < *condition* > (which must be a constant integer expression) to be evaluated by the preprocessor during text transcription. If the condition is satisfied (i.e. its result is non-zero), then the following lines of text are transcribed into the preprocessed program (including any text substitution required). Transcription continues until a line is encountered commencing with **#else**, **#elif**, or **#endif**.

The (optional) **#else** directive has a similar connotation to **else** in a conditional statement; in this case, the effect is that the preprocessor tran-

```
#if COMPUTER == HP

#define BITS32 int
#define BITS16 short

#elif COMPUTER == IBMpc

#define BITS32 long
#define BITS16 int

#else

#define BITS32 int
#define BITS16 short

#endif

void check(int x, int y)
{
#ifdef TRACE
    printf("trace output...x= %d, y= %d\n",x,y);
#endif
    if (x>y) f(x);
    else f(y);
}
```

Figure 5.8   An example of conditional inclusion

scribes *either* the text between #if and #else, *or* the text between #else
and the directive #endif that terminates the control sequence. Chains of
conditional sequences can be defined using directives of the form #else if
< *condition* >, which can also be contracted to #elif < *condition* >, and
the whole chain concluded with a single #endif.

Figure 5.8 shows the use of conditional compilation to deal with an
aspect of machine-dependency, by defining macro-names for type identifiers
that are preprocessed into actual type-names appropriate for the target
computer. Only one of the three pairs of definitions, for the macro-names
BITS32 and BITS16, is effective in any one compilation.

The final part of Figure 5.8 illustrates a special case of conditional compilation. In this case, we wish the **printf()** function call to be included in the text of the function **check()** *only* if the name **TRACE** has previously been defined (using a **#define** directive), and has not been undefined using **#undef**. The **#ifdef** directive is a special form of **#if**, used for this purpose. We could also have written this as:

```
#if defined (TRACE)
```

The expression **defined** ($<$ *name* $>$), evaluated during preprocessing, delivers the result 1 (TRUE) if the name has been defined, or 0 otherwise. **#ifdef** is a contraction of this, and we can also use **#ifndef** to mean 'if not defined'.

Predefined macros

The standard ANSI C preprocessor has five predefined macros which may be used. Each macro-name is preceded and succeeded by two underscore characters, and these names may not be undefined using **#undef**. The macro-names and their purpose are illustrated in Figure 5.9, while Figure 5.10 illustrates their use, and the output produced by the program using them.

Macro	Its expansion
DATE	The current date as a string
TIME	The current time as a string
FILE	The current file name as a string
LINE	The current line number as an integer
STDC	A non-zero integer when the compiler conforms to ANSI Standard C

Figure 5.9   ANSI C predefined macros

5.3 Multi-file programs

As we have seen, the C language and environment provides support for us to divide programs between separate files, which may be combined textually at the preprocessing stage (using the **#include** directive) or compiled separately and brought together by the linker. There are often good reasons for doing this: this kind of program **modularization** allows us to develop and test independent parts of the program separately, and to reuse functions in more than one program.

```
/* This program illustrates the use of predefined macros. */
#include <stdio.h>
main()
{
   printf("The time is %s\n",__TIME__);
   printf("The date is %s\n",__DATE__);
   printf("The file name is %s\n",__FILE__);
   printf("The line number is %d\n",__LINE__);
   if (__STDC__) printf("ANSI standard adhered to\n");
   else printf("not ANSI C\n");
}
```

Output from the program:

```
The time is 17:30:05
The date is Mar 14 1991
The file name is predef.c
The line number is 9
ANSI standard adhered to
```

Figure 5.10   An example of the use of predefined macros

Separate compilation of functions can, however, introduce some problems. In particular, if a function refers to a global variable, then it is necessary for that variable to be declared within the same compilation unit as the function. If *two* separately compiled functions refer to the same global variable, then it is necessary for the variable to be declared in both compilation units, which would, ordinarily, lead to an error as a result of the multiple definition of the same symbol.

The problem is resolved by the use of an explicit declaration of the variable as being of storage class **extern**. Suppose that two functions, to be compiled separately, both wish to make use of an integer variable, **count**. In one of the files, **count** must be defined with a global declaration of the form:

$$\text{int count;}$$

which not only declares the name **count**, for use within that file, but also causes space to be allocated for the variable. In any other separately compiled file that refers to count, there must be included a declaration:

extern int count;

This form of declaration allows the variable identifier to be used within the compilation unit, but does not set aside any storage space for it, so that when the two object files are linked, all references to count will be mapped onto the single defined variable.

Figure 5.11 shows a program that we have chosen to divide between two files. In Figure 5.11(a), the file *extern.c* contains the main program function, which makes reference to the function error(). Because this function is not defined within this file, an extern declaration of the function name is included. Similarly, the function error(), defined within the file *error.c* (Figure 5.11(b)), contains references to the global variables error_number and title that are defined in the file *extern.c*. To enable the contents of the file *error.c* to be compiled successfully, it includes extern declarations of these variables.

An extern declaration may be included either outside the body of a function, as in these examples, or inside, if it is required that the scope of the declaration be confined to the function body. No 'multiple declaration' error arises if an extern declaration of a variable occurs in the same file as the definition of a variable, so that, if the two files of Figure 5.11(a) and (b) were concatenated, they could still be compiled successfully. This also means that extern declarations can be used, within a single file, to 'predeclare' variables that are defined later in the file. Notice also that when an extern declaration is made for an array, it is not necessary to define the array size.

Using the hypothetical commands introduced in Section 5.1, we could compile, link and execute the program defined in Figure 5.11 with the following sequence:

```
$ ccomp extern.c
$ ccomp error.c
$ link extern.o error.o
$ extern.ex

input quotient and divisor(* to end) 6 5
division=1
input quotient and divisor(* to end) 4 0
error 1 met in program 'To show how extern works'
input quotient and divisor(* to end) 1 7*
division=0
```

```
#include <stdio.h>

extern void error();

char title [] = "To show how extern works";
int error_number;

main()
{
   int quotient,divisor;
   char terminator='g';

   while (terminator!='*')
   {
      printf("input quotient and divisor(* to end) ");
      scanf("%d%d%c",&quotient,&divisor,&terminator);
      if (divisor==0) error(1);
      else printf("division=%d\n",quotient/divisor);
   }
}
```

(a) File *extern.c*

```
#include <stdio.h>

extern int error_number;
extern char title [];

void error(int e_num)
{
   error_number=e_num;
   printf("error %d met in program '%s'\n",e_num,title);
}
```

(b) File *error.c*

Figure 5.11   An example of a program split between two files

Undeclared functions

In Figure 5.11, the function **error()** was declared with an **extern** declaration in the file *extern.c* prior to its definition in the file *error.c*. In fact, unlike variables, it is possible for functions to be used prior to their declaration. When this occurs, the compiler assumes that the function returns a value of type **int**, and does not attempt to check either the number of arguments or their types. If the function is declared subsequently in the same file to return a result other than an **int**, then a compilation error is recorded. If the function is compiled separately, however, or if there is a mismatch of the types or number of arguments, then an error in execution is likely to ensue.

```
#include <stdio.h>
main()
{
    double a;

    a = show();
    printf("%f",a);
}
```

(a) File *miss1.c*

```
double show()
{
    return (6.7);
}
```

(b) File *miss2.c*

Figure 5.12   Example of a function result mismatch

Figure 5.12 illustrates a simple instance. Here, the files *miss1.c* and *miss2.c* can be compiled separately without errors being reported; however, in the compilation of the function **main()** it is assumed that the function **show()** returns a result of type **int** (which is then converted to type **double**). When the program is executed, the actual result returned by **show()** is of type **double**, and this value is misinterpreted, to produce

```
#include <stdio.h>

extern double show(void);

main()
{
   double a;

   a = show();
   printf("%f",a);
}
```

(a) File *cormiss1.c*

```
double show()
{
   return 6.7;
}
```

(b) File *cormiss2.c*

Figure 5.13   Correcting the mismatch

a spurious result in main().

The problem can be avoided by the use of an **extern** declaration to declare a **function prototype** for show(). Figure 5.13 shows how this is done. Function prototypes were introduced in Chapter 3, as a way of declaring the characteristics of a function prior to its full definition. In this case, we are using the **extern** form of the declaration to declare a prototype for a function that is defined in a separate file.

Figure 5.14 shows another kind of mismatch; in this case, the parameter specification of the function prototype declared in the file *miss3.c* is different from that of the actual function definition in *miss4.c*. Because the files are compiled separately, the compiler detects no error, giving rise to incorrect results at run-time.

Had the function prototype been declared at the start of each file, the compiler would have detected the mismatch. For this reason, when linking

```
#include <stdio.h>

extern int show(float);

main()
{
    int a;

    a = show(7);
    printf("%d",a);
}
```

(a) File *miss3.c*

```
int show(int a)
{
    return a;
}
```

(b) File *miss4.c*

Figure 5.14   Example of a function argument mismatch

a program from a set of separately compiled units, it is often convenient and good practice to create one 'header' file to contain **extern** declarations and function prototypes for all global variables and functions. If this header file is included in every program file, this ensures that all global references are checked correctly during compilation. In this case, we might create a header file *mydefs.h* to contain both the library header file *stdio.h* and the **extern** declaration of show() (Figure 5.15).

Inclusion of this header file, using the directive **#include "mydefs.h"**, in the files *cormiss3.c* and *cormiss4.c* (Figure 5.16) ensures that the mismatch between the function prototype and its definition is detected by the compiler. Notice again that it is not incorrect to include a declaration of an **extern** function or variable in the same file as the actual definition of the object declared.

File *mydefs.h*

`#include <stdio.h>`

`extern int show(float);`

Figure 5.15   A header file

```
#include "mydefs.h"

main()
{
   int a;

   a = show(7);
   printf("%d",a);
}
```

(a) File *cormiss3.c*

```
#include "mydefs.h"

int show(int a)
{
   return a ;
}
```

(b) File *cormiss4.c*

Figure 5.16   Using a header file

5.4   The standard library

We have made reference several times to the standard library of functions that is provided as part of any complete implementation of ANSI C. Associated with this library is a set of standard header files that contain the necessary **extern** declarations and function prototypes to enable these functions to be used correctly; for example, as we have seen, if a program requires to make use of any of the standard input and output functions, it must include the header file *stdio.h*. As well as the standard input and output functions, however, the library contains a variety of useful functions for other purposes; these are conveniently grouped into a number of sets, associated with each of which is a different standard header.

String handling functions: string.h

Recall that a string in C is an array of characters, terminated by a null character, which is accessed via a pointer (**char** *). The standard library contains functions to perform string operations such as copying, comparison, and concatenation. To use these functions, the standard header *string.h* must be included, i.e.:

```
#include <string.h>
```

As an example, the function:

```
char *strcat(char *s1, const char *s2)
```

will concatenate the strings **s1** and **s2**, assigning the result to **s1**. Here, and in general with string handling functions, it is the programmer's responsibility to ensure that the destination string (**s1** in this case) has been defined to be large enough to contain the result without overwriting other information. The function returns a pointer to **s1**.

The function:

```
char *strncat(char *s1, const char *s2, size_t n)
```

is similar, except that in this case only the first **n** characters of **s2** are appended to **s1**. The type of the parameter **n** is defined to be **size_t**, which is the type of the result returned by the **sizeof** operator; the actual type to which this corresponds is defined in a header file, *stddef.h*, and is usually **unsigned int**. The *stddef.h* header contains a number of definitions of implementation-dependent characteristics of the library functions; it is not necessary to include *stddef.h* explicitly in the program text, however, as it is included where necessary in the appropriate library header.

The other functions in *string.h* have, in general, similar characteristics. For example:

```
int strcmp(const char *s1,*s2)
```

performs a lexicographic comparison of the two strings, returning a value 0 if they are equal, <0 if s1 precedes s2, or >0 if s2 precedes s1. The form of this result can sometimes lead to error: the result of strcmp(buffer,"FRED") will be 0 (i.e. FALSE) when the strings are equal, so a construction such as:

```
if (strcmp(buffer,"FRED"))
```

can be misleading.

```
int strncmp(const char *s1, const char *s2, size_t n)
```

is similar, but compares only the first n characters of each string.

Briefly, the remaining functions referenced in *string.h* are as follows:

```
char *strcpy(char *s1,const char *s2)
```
Copy s2 (including its terminating character) into s1.

```
char *strncpy(char *s1,const char *s2, size_t n)
```
Copy n characters of s2 into s1.

```
size_t strlen(const char *s)
```
Return length of s, not including terminator.

```
char *strchr(const char *s,char c)
```
Return a pointer to the first occurrence of the character c in s.

```
char *strrchr(const char *s,char c)
```
Return a pointer to the last occurrence of c in s.

```
size_t strspn(const char *s1,*s2)
```
Return the length of the leading substring of s1 consisting of characters from s2.

```
size_t strcspn(const char *s1,*s2)
```
Return the length of the leading substring of s1 consisting of characters not in s2.

```
char *strpbrk(const char *s1,*s2)
```
Return a pointer to the first occurrence in the string s1 of any character found in s2.

```
char *strstr(const char *s1,*s2)
```
Return a pointer to the first occurrence of s2 in s1.

```
char *strerror(size_t n)
```
Return a pointer to a string corresponding to error number **n**.

```
char *strtok(char *s1,const char *s2)
```
Return a pointer to a token in **s1** delimited by a character from **s2**. (The first call of **strtok** delivers a pointer to the first such token, whose delimiting character is overwritten with the null character. Subsequent calls, using a null value for **s1**, return pointers to succeeding tokens in turn.)

```
void *memmove(void *s1,const void *s2,size_t n)
```
Move n characters from the memory array **s2** into **s1**.

```
void *memcpy(void *s1,const void *s2,size_t n)
```
Move n characters from **s2** into the *non-overlapping* area **s1**.

```
int memcmp(const void *s1,*s2,size_t n)
```
Compare first **n** characters of **s1** and **s2**.

```
void *memchr(const void *s,unsigned char c,size_t n)
```
Return a pointer to the first occurrence of **c** in the first **n** characters of **s**.

```
void *memset(void *s,unsigned char c,size_t n)
```
Copy **c** into the first **n** characters of **s**.

Finally, beware of some common errors which can arise from the use of string handling functions. Some functions (for example **strlen()**) do not make use of the string terminating character, while others, such as **strcpy()**, do so. Consequently, a sequence such as

```
          char *ptr = malloc(strlen(buffer));
          strcpy(ptr,buffer);
```

will allocate one byte too few for the copy of the existing string.

A more general mistake is to use as a parameter to a string function a pointer variable whose value has not been initialized. For example:

```
               strcpy(ptr,buffer);
```

will have undefined and probably disastrous effects if the destination string pointer **ptr** has been declared but not assigned to point to a free area of store.

Conversion routines

The standard library contains a number of functions to perform conversions between textual and binary representations of numbers. Most of these

are included in the set associated with the header file *stdlib.h* which also
includes functions such as `malloc()`.

The function:

```
double strtod(const char *str,char **ptr)
```

is used to convert leading numeric characters in `str` into a numeric value
of type `double`. Leading 'white space' characters are ignored. After completion of the function, `ptr` references the address of the next character in
`str` following the number representation.

```
long strtol(const char *str,char **ptr,int base)
```

offers a more general conversion, using the numeric base given as a parameter (in the range 2–36). If base 0 is given, then the conversion will take
place according to the leading characters of `str`: the prefix 0x or 0X is
taken to imply a hexadecimal number, 0 to imply an octal number, and
any other prefix implies a decimal number.

```
unsigned long strtoul()
```

is similar to `strtol()` but produces an `unsigned long` result.

Simpler numeric conversions are provided by the functions `atoi()`,
`atol()` and `atof()`, which convert a (decimal) string to `int`, `long` and
`double` respectively, returning the value produced as the result of the function call.

Two functions included in the standard input–output header, *stdio.h*,
may also be used to perform conversions between numeric and textual
forms. Recall that the functions `printf()` and `scanf()`, described in Section 2.3, provide for formatted output and input, converting between numeric and textual representations in the process. The functions `sprintf()`
and `sscanf()` are similar, except that in these cases the text string that is
created (in the case of `sprintf()`) or converted (in the case of `sscanf()`)
is contained in memory rather than being read or printed.

Thus:

```
int sprintf(char *s,const char *format,< argument list >)
```

will convert a sequence of arguments into a text string, in the form determined by the format string, storing the result as the string s. Likewise:

```
int sscanf(const char *s,const char *format,< argument list >)
```

'reads' the string s as data, according to the format specification, and stores
the resulting values in the variables specified in the argument list.

Character testing functions

A set of functions associated with the library header *ctype.h* provide simple tests on character values. These functions (which are sometimes implemented as library **macros**) take as a parameter an `int` value (representing a character) and return the value TRUE (non-zero) or FALSE (zero) depending on whether the character code supplied satisfies the test.

```
int isalpha(int c)
```
Test if c is a letter.

```
int isupper(int c)
```
Test if c is an upper-case letter.

```
int islower(int c)
```
Test if c is a lower-case letter.

```
int isdigit(int c)
```
Test if c is a decimal digit.

```
int isalnum(int c)
```
Test if c is alphabetic or numeric.

```
int isxdigit(int c)
```
Test if c is a hexadecimal digit.

```
int isprint(int c)
```
Test if c is a printable character.

```
int isgraph(int c)
```
Test if c is a printable character (excluding space).

```
int isspace(int c)
```
Test if c is a 'white space' character, e.g. space, newline, formfeed, carriage return, tab, vertical tab.

```
int ispunct(int c)
```
Test if c is a punctuation character (printable character not including letters, digits, space).

```
int iscntrl(int c)
```
Test if c is a control character.

Also declared in the header *ctype.h* are two functions to perform character conversions:

```
int toupper(int c)
```
Converts lower-case letter c to upper case.

```
int tolower(int c)
```
Converts upper-case letter c to lower case.

Dealing with functions with variable numbers of parameters

A number of definitions provided by the library header *stdarg.h* enable us to write functions with variable-length parameter lists. We can declare a function of this kind with a formal parameter list concluding with a sequence of three dots, thus:

```
int somefunc(int firstparam,...)
```

This declaration specifies that somefunc() has a first parameter named firstparam, and an undefined number of other parameters, of undefined type. The '...' specification, when used, must be the last element in the parameter list. Functions such as scanf() and printf(), defined in the standard library, have this form.

In order to refer to the *actual* parameters that are supplied when a call of somefunc() is made, the function must declare a variable of type va_list:

```
va_list paramptr;
```

The type va_list, defined in the header *stdarg.h*, is used to declare a pointer to the parameters of somefunc(). The pointer must first be initialized, using the macro va_start():

```
va_start (paramptr,firstparam);
```

This call sets paramptr to refer to the *first* parameter following the named parameter, firstparam; that is, it will point to the first unnamed parameter in the actual parameter list.

Thereafter, actual parameters may be extracted from the parameter list using successive invocations of the macro va_arg(). Thus:

```
nextarg = va_arg (paramptr,int);
```

will obtain the next parameter (of type int) and advance paramptr to refer to its successor. To use this macro successfully, it is necessary that the function has some means of knowing the types of successive parameters; for example, in the case of printf(), this is provided via the format specification.

Finally, before the function terminates, the macro va_end() must be invoked:

```
void va_end (va_list paramptr);
```

to conclude the sequence.

Figure 5.17 is an illustration of the use of this facility. The function **average()** computes the average of a variable number of parameters, the actual number being given as the first parameter, **num**. Although the type of the result of **average()** is **float**, its internal arithmetic is carried out using the type **double**; the reason for this is that literal values such as 11.7, 12.0, etc., included as actual parameters, are stored as type **double**. Consequently, the invocation **va_arg(next_ptr,float)** would lead to only part of the number representation being obtained.

Input and output using files

In Chapter 2, we introduced some standard functions for performing input and output operations, including in particular the formatted transput functions **printf()** and **scanf()**. These functions operate on input and output **streams** that are associated with particular peripheral devices in the configuration of the C implementation in use. The input stream associated with **scanf()** is the standard input stream **stdin**, and the output stream associated with **printf()** is the standard output stream **stdout**; they are typically configured to refer to the user terminal keyboard and screen respectively.

More generally, input and output operations take place via streams which may be associated either with physical devices or with **files**. For this purpose, a special data type **FILE** is defined in the library header *stdio.h*. The nature of this type is implementation-dependent, but we do not need to know the details: we always reference a **FILE** through a pointer variable, which is equivalent to a **stream**. We now introduce the library functions required to make use of files; an example of the use of files will be found in the next chapter.

To use a file, it must first be opened using the library function **fopen()**:

```
FILE *fopen(const char *filename,const char *use)
```

The first parameter of this function is a text string which will be associated in some system-dependent way with an external file or device—i.e. it will typically be the name of a file in the user's own directory. The second parameter defines the way in which the file is to be used, by one of a number of use codes:

"**r**"   open for reading only
"**w**"   open for writing only

```
/*
 *This program illustrates the use of a variable number of
 * arguments. The function average averages a set of
 * numbers. The first argument tells how many numbers there
 * are to average.
 */

#include <stdio.h>
#include <stdarg.h>

float average(int num, ...);

main()
{
    printf("My average 100 metre time: %f\n",
               average(4,11.7,12.0,11.8,12.3));

    printf("My average 400 metre time: %f\n",
                average(3,62.1,59.7,60.3));
}

/*----------------------------------------------------------*/

float average(int num, ...)
{
    int i;
    double tally = 0.0;
    va_list next_ptr;

    va_start(next_ptr, num);
    for (i=0; i<num; i++)
        tally += va_arg(next_ptr, double);
    va_end(next_ptr);
    return (float)tally/num;
}
```

Figure 5.17   A function with a variable number of parameters

"a"   open for appending only
"r+"   open for reading, writing and amending
"w+"   open for overwriting, destroying previous contents, and reading
"a+"   open for appending, reading and writing

A call of fopen() returns a pointer to the opened file, i.e. a stream on which input and/or output operations can take place using further function calls. If for any reason the attempt to open the file fails (if, for example, an attempt is made to open for reading a file which does not exist) the call of fopen() will return a NULL pointer.

Figure 5.18 shows a typical sequence for opening a file. Notice that the declaration:

FILE *read_file;

has declared a pointer to a FILE, which is assigned the value returned from the call of fopen(). The identifier read_file will subsequently be used to refer to the stream in performing operations on the file opened.

```
#include <stdio.h>
  FILE *read_file;

  if ( (read_file=fopen("myfile.data","r"))==NULL)
  {
     printf("unable to open 'myfile.data' for reading\n");
     exit(1);
  }
```

Figure 5.18   An example of opening a file

An alternative to fopen() is freopen():

FILE *freopen (const char *filename,const char *use, FILE
                        *stream)

which associates the named stream with the file opened.

Files opened are closed automatically when the program terminates normally, or through a call of exit(). However, it is sometimes necessary to close files explicitly during the execution of the program, using the function fclose():

int fclose (FILE *stream)

which returns the value 0 if the file has been closed successfully. Thus, the
file opened in Figure 5.18 would be closed by the call:

`fclose (read_file);`

File read and write operations

When a file has been opened, transput operations to and from the file can
proceed in much the same way as standard input and output operations, using functions that refer to the stream associated with the file. The functions
fscanf() and fprintf() are the file transput equivalents of the formatted
transput functions scanf() and printf() which were introduced in Chapter 2. Thus:

```
int fscanf(FILE *stream,const char *format,< argument list >)
int fprintf(FILE *stream,const char *format,< argument list >)
```

The format strings used follow the conventions defined for scanf() and
printf() in Chapter 2, and the functions have just the same effects except
that in this case the input or output takes place using the file associated
with the stream parameter.

Simpler functions are available for reading and writing single characters:

```
int fgetc(FILE *stream)
```
reads a single character from stream.

```
int fputc(int c,FILE *stream)
```
writes the character c to stream.

Both of these functions are also available in alternative versions that
may be implemented as **macros**:

```
int getc(FILE *stream)
```
reads a single character from stream.

```
int putc(int c,FILE *stream)
```
writes the character c to stream.

In most cases, using getc() and putc() produces identical results to
those obtained using fgetc() and fputc(). In general, using a macro leads
to faster execution (sometimes at the cost of a larger object program) than
the use of the corresponding function; however, care is sometimes needed
to ensure that there are no unwanted side-effects produced from the use of
the macro.

All these functions return the value of a character that was read or
written. If the file referred to is empty (on reading) or full (on writing) the

EOF character (defined in the header file *stdio.h*) is returned.

Functions that read from or write to a file implicitly advance a pointer to the character-position within the file, so that, for example, two successive getc() calls fetch successive characters from the file. It is possible to restore the last character read, stepping back the pointer, using the function ungetc():

```
ungetc(int c,FILE *stream)
```
Restore the character c to the file from which it was read.

ungetc() may be used to replace the last character read using getc(), fgetc(), fscanf() or any other input function. Usually, it is only possible to replace *one* character in this way.

Functions are also provided for input and output of **strings**:

```
char *fgets(char *s,int n,FILE *stream)
int fputs(char *s,FILE *stream)
```

fgets() reads at most n-1 characters up to and including the next newline character, storing them in the string s, terminated by the '\0' character. The function returns the address of the string, or NULL if end-of-file is encountered. It is the responsibility of the programmer to ensure that the string is large enough to contain the characters read.

fputs() writes the string s, terminated by the null character, to the stream given. The null terminator is not itself output. The function returns the result EOF if an error arises, or 0 otherwise.

Just as getchar() and putchar() are equivalents of getc() and putc() for use with stdin and stdout respectively, so the functions gets() and puts() read and write strings using the standard channels.

```
char *gets(char *s)
```
reads a line from the standard input channel, replacing the terminating newline with a null terminator.

```
int puts(const char *s)
```
writes the string to the standard output channel, terminated by a newline character.

Binary transput

So far we have described input and output of textual data only. The functions fread() and fwrite() perform transput of binary values:

```
size_t fread(void *ptr,size_t size,size_t nitems,
                                         FILE *stream)
size_t fwrite(const void *ptr,size_t size,size_t nitems,
                                         FILE *stream)
```

Recall that **size_t** is an implementation-dependent type, which is usually equivalenced to **unsigned int**. The functions take parameters **nitems** and **size**, of this type, which define respectively the number of values to be read or written, and the size in bytes of each value. **ptr** is a pointer to the area of memory used to store the data. The number of items transferred is returned as the result of the function call; this will be less than **nitems** if end-of-file is reached or another error condition arises.

In some systems, binary files and files containing textual information need to be treated differently, although this is not so in the case of UNIX. If it is required to open a file for binary transput only, the 'use' parameter of **fopen()** is given the suffix 'b'. Thus:

```
fopen("binary-file","rb")
```

opens the named file for reading binary data.

An example of the use of files

Figure 5.19 illustrates the use of some of the functions we have been describing in this chapter. The program takes as command-line arguments the names of two files, on which are opened the streams **in_file** and **out_file**. Text is copied from **in_file** to **out_file**, with leading space characters removed from the start of each line.

The program starts with two **#include** directives, for the library headers *stdio.h* and *ctype.h*. All the input and output routines require the header *stdio.h*, while *ctype.h* is needed for the function **isspace()**, used in this program. Notice the use of the function prototype for **remove_lead_space()**, declared at the start of the program.

Random access files

So far, we have implicitly assumed that a file takes the form of a serial device to which data may be written in sequence, and from which data may be read in the same sequence. The position in the file from which, for example, a character is read by **getc()**, is determined by a pointer which is advanced as each character is read in sequence.

It is possible, however, to change the value of this position-pointer by explicit function calls, allowing us to determine at what point within the

```
/*
 * This program illustrates the use of files.
 */
#include <stdio.h>
#include <ctype.h>

void remove_lead_space(FILE *,FILE *);

main(int argc, char *argv[])
{
    FILE *in_file, *out_file;

    if (argc != 3)
    {
        printf("You should have 2 arguments\n");
        exit(1);
    }
    if ( (in_file=fopen(argv[1],"r")) == NULL)
    {
        printf("Unable to open '%s' for reading\n",argv[1]);
        exit(1);
    }
    if ( (out_file=fopen(argv[2],"w")) == NULL)
    {
        printf("Unable to open '%s' for writing\n",argv[2]);
        exit(1);
    }

    remove_lead_space(in_file,out_file);

    fclose(in_file); fclose(out_file);
}
/*-----------------------------------------------------------*/
```

```
/*
 *This function removes 'white space' characters at the
 * start of lines. It takes two arguments:
 * f_in a FILE pointer to the file to be read
 * f_out a FILE pointer to the file to be written to.
 */
void remove_lead_space(FILE *f_in, FILE *f_out)
{
    char c;

    c=getc(f_in);
    while (c != EOF)
    {
        while(isspace(c) && c!='\n') c=getc(f_in);

        while(c!='\n' && c != EOF)
        {
            putc(c,f_out); c=getc(f_in);
        }
        if (c != EOF)
        {
            putc(c,f_out); c=getc(f_in);
        }
    }
}
```

Figure 5.19   Using files

file we wish to recommence reading or writing. The function `ftell()` tells
us the *current* byte position within the file, relative to the start of the file:

$$\text{long ftell(FILE *stream)}$$

The value thus returned may be stored, and used subsequently as a parameter to `fseek()`:

$$\text{int fseek(FILE *stream,long offset,int start\_point)}$$

Here, the value of `offset` defines the point in the file to which the position-
pointer will be set. The parameter `start_point` defines the base from

which this offset is calculated, which may be one of three constants defined in *stdio.h*: SEEK_SET, which defines the start of the file, SEEK_END (end-of-file) or SEEK_CUR (current position). Typically:

```
fseek(text_file,previous_pos,SEEK_SET);
```
Reset to a previously saved position.

```
fseek(text_file,0L,SEEK_END);
```
Set to end-of-file.

```
fseek(bin_file,10L,SEEK_CUR);
```
Advance pointer in binary file by 10 byte positions.

fseek() returns a non-zero value to indicate an error. After a successful call of fseek(), reading or writing from or to the file continues from the newly-defined position. The rewind() function may be used to reposition at the start of the file:

```
void rewind(FILE *stream)
```

An alternative pair of file positioning functions is fgetpos() and fsetpos().

```
int fgetpos(FILE *stream,fpos_t *ptr)
int fsetpos(FILE *stream,const fpos_t *ptr)
```

fgetpos() returns the current absolute file position, as a value of the type fpos_t that is defined when *stdio.h* is used. This value (ptr) may be used subsequently in a call of fsetpos() to reposition the file at this point. The two functions return a non-zero result in cases of error.

Errors

We have already discussed the standard input and output streams stdin and stdout used by functions such as scanf() and putchar(). One other standard stream is defined: stderr defines the stream on which any system error messages will appear. Usually this will be the same device as stdout, but it is possible for the user to reassign this to a file, for example using the freopen() function.

Many library functions report an error not by printing out an error message but by returning some specific error indication that may be tested. In some cases, an **error number** is also recorded in the system variable errno, which may be used to obtain more information about the error. The function:

```
char *strerror(size_t errno)
```

returns a pointer to a character string associated with the error number
errno (which may then, for example, be printed). This character string
is an implementation-defined error message appropriate for the given error
number. **strerror()** is declared in the header *string.h*. Alternatively:

void perror(const char *s)

defined in *stdio.h*, prints the string **s** followed by the error message associated with the current value of **errno**.

Other associated functions are:

    int ferror(FILE *stream)
Returns non-zero if a stream error has been recorded.

    int feof(FILE *stream)
Returns non-zero if end-of-file has been reached.

    void clearerr(FILE *stream)
Clears the stream end-of-file and error indicators.

Other input and output functions

A few miscellaneous functions included via the header *stdio.h* are mentioned
briefly here, for completeness.

    vprintf(const char *format,va_list paramptr)
    vfprintf(FILE *stream,const char *format,va_list paramptr)
    vsprintf(char *s,const char *format,va_list paramptr)

These functions are identical to **printf()**, **fprintf()** and **sprintf()** respectively, except that instead of a variable-length parameter list (i.e. a
parameter specification of the form '...'), the functions are provided with
a single parameter of type **va_list**. This type, declared in *stdarg.h*, provides a pointer to a variable-length list of parameters. The macros supplied
via *stdarg.h* enable this pointer to be set to refer to the list of parameters
of the current function, which may then be passed on directly to be used
by **vprintf()**, **vfprintf()** or **vsprintf()**.

    int setvbuf(FILE *stream,char *buffer,int mode,size_t size)

Normally, file transput is buffered in a system-dependent way. If it is necessary to take control of this, the function **setvbuf()** must be called before
any read or write operations are performed on the stream, to define the
mode of buffering required: _IOFBF (full buffering), _IOLBF (line buffering of text files) or _IONBF (no buffering). The parameter **buffer** may be

null, or may point to an array (of size **size**) that will be used as the buffer.

int setbuf(FILE *stream,char *buffer)
Resets buffering; if the buffer is NULL, buffering is turned off, otherwise full buffering is restored.

int fflush(FILE *stream)
(On an output stream) causes any output remaining in the buffer to be written.

char *tmpnam(char *s)
This function may be used to generate a sequence of different names for temporary files. With a NULL parameter, it returns a pointer to a string which is not the name of an existing file. With a parameter **s**, this string will also be stored in the array given (which must be large enough to contain a string of length **L_tmpnam**, defined in *stddef.h*).

FILE *tmpfile(void)
Creates a temporary file, with access mode '**w+b**', and returns a stream for this file (as if opened via **fopen()**). The file thus created is deleted when the file is closed or the program terminates.

int remove(const char *filename)
Removes the named file.

int rename(const char *filename,const char *newname)
Renames the file.

Mathematical functions

ANSI C provides the usual set of mathematical functions, here included via the header *math.h*. In general, the argument 'x' of a mathematical function is of type **double**, as is the result returned. Figure 5.20 summarizes these functions.

In addition to the functions declared in the header *math.h*, a number of mathematical functions are declared in the 'utility' header *stdlib.h*. These are the following:

int abs(int n)
Absolute value of an integer.

long labs(long n)
Absolute value of a long integer.

div_t div(int n,int m)
Returns the quotient and remainder of n/m, as integers (**quot** and **rem**).

```
ldiv_t ldiv(long n,m)
```
Returns the quotient and remainder of n/m, as long integers (quot and rem).

The last two functions return a result which is a **structure**: this is a topic that is explained in the next chapter.

Function	Result
sin(x)	sine
cos(x)	cosine
tan(x)	tangent
asin(x)	$\sin^{-1}(x)$ (-1<=x<=1)
acos(x)	$\cos^{-1}(x)$ (-1<=x<=1)
atan(x)	$\tan^{-1}(x)$
atan2(x,y)	$\tan^{-1}(x/y)$
sinh(x)	hyperbolic sine
cosh(x)	hyperbolic cosine
tanh(x)	hyperbolic tangent
exp(x)	e^x
log(x)	log to base e (x>0)
log10(x)	log to base 10 (x>0)
pow(x,y)	x^y (for negative x, y must be integral)
sqrt(x)	$\sqrt{x}$ (x>=0)
ceil(x)	smallest integer value which is >= x
floor(x)	largest integer value <= x
fabs(x)	absolute value
ldexp(x,n)	$x * 2^n$ (integer n)
frexp(x,int *exponent)	returns the normalized mantissa of x, and stores the binary exponent
modf(x,double *ip)	returns the fractional part of x, and stores its integer part in ip
fmod(x,y)	remainder of x/y

Figure 5.20   Mathematical functions

Miscellaneous functions

Finally, we will make brief mention here of a number of other functions defined in the standard library. Most of these are declared in the header *stdlib.h*. The functions malloc() and free(), used in memory-allocation, were introduced in Chapter 3. Other memory-allocation functions are:

```
void *calloc(size_t n,size_t s)
```
Allocates space for n objects of size s which are initialized to zero.

```
void *realloc(void *p,size_t size)
```
Extends or contracts the memory space pointed to by p, by the amount defined as **size**.

As with **malloc()**, these functions return a pointer to the space allocated. Note again the use of the type **size_t** for the function parameters; this is the type that is returned as the result of the **sizeof** operator, and used in a range of different functions requiring an unsigned integer parameter.

The conversion functions **strod()**, **strol()**, **stroul()**, **atoi()**, **atol()** and **atof()**, and the arithmetic functions **abs()**, **labs()**, **div()** and **ldiv()**, have been described earlier in this section. The other functions declared in *stdlib.h* are as follows:

```
int rand(void)
```
Returns a random number in the range 0 to **RAND_MAX**.

```
void srand(unsigned int i)
```
Uses i to seed a new random number sequence for **rand()**.

```
int atexit(void(*fn)(void))
```
This function takes as a parameter a pointer to a function, that is recorded by the system as a function to be called on program termination (pointers to functions are described in Chapter 7). A number of such functions may be defined, and are called in reverse order of recording.

```
void exit(int status)
```
Terminates program execution, after calling any **atexit()** functions.

```
void abort(void)
```
Used for abnormal program termination.

```
int system(const char *s)
```
Invokes a system call, using the string s. The effect is system-dependent.

```
char *getenv(const char *name)
```
Returns the (system-dependent) environment string associated with **name**.

```
void *bsearch(const void *key,const void *table,size_t n,
size_t size,int(*cmpfunc)(const void *val,const void *entry))
```
Searches a table of n elements, sorted into ascending order, for a match to **key**, using the comparison function **cmpfunc()**. This must compare the values of its two parameters, a key value and a table entry, returning 0 if

they are equal, negative if the key is less than the entry, or positive if it
is greater. bsearch() returns a pointer to the item found, or NULL if no
match is found.

```
void qsort(void *table,size_t n,size_t size,
           int(*cmpfunc)(const void *,const void *))
```
Sorts a table of n elements into ascending order, using the comparison
function cmpfunc() (defined as for bsearch()) to define the ordering relationship. The application of qsort() is illustrated in an example program
in Chapter 7.

A number of functions for obtaining the current date and time are declared in the header *time.h*:

```
int tm_hour()
```
Returns hours since midnight.

```
int tm_min()
```
Returns minutes in current hour.

```
int tm_sec()
```
Returns seconds in current minute.

```
int tm_year()
```
Returns years since 1900.

```
int tm_mon()
```
Returns months since January (January = 0).

```
int tm_mday()
```
Returns day in the month.

```
int tm_wday()
```
Returns day in the week (Sunday = 0).

```
int tm_yday()
```
Returns day in the year (Jan 1st = 0).

```
int tm_isdst()
```
Returns positive if daylight saving time (summertime) is in effect, 0 if not,
negative if not known.

```
clock_t clock(void)
```
Returns the current processor time (-1 if not available); dividing the answer
by the constant CLK_TCK gives a time in seconds.

```
time_t time(time_t *ptr)
```
Returns the current calendar time, as a value of type time_t.

`time_t mktime(struct tm *ptr)`
Converts the local time, recorded in the structure *ptr, into calendar time
of type `time_t`.

`double difftime(time_t time2,time_t time1)`
Returns `time2-time1` in seconds.

`char *asctime(const struct tm *ptr)`
Converts the time in the structure *ptr into a string of the form (weekday,
month, day, time, year).

`struct tm *localtime(const time_t *ptr)`
Converts calendar time into local time.

`char *ctime(const time_t *ptr)`
Converts calendar time into local time, as a printable string.

`struct tm *gmtime(const time_t *ptr)`
Converts calendar time into Coordinated Universal Time.

`size_t strftime(char *s,size_t smax,const char *format,`
`                const struct tm *ptr)`
Formats the time recorded in the structure *ptr according to the format
given, placing the result in the string s, of maximum size smax. The for-
matting copies characters from the structure, replacing all those prefixed %
as follows:

%a	weekday name (short form)
%A	weekday name
%b	month name (short form)
%B	month name
%c	local date and time
%d	day of the month
%H	hour (24-hour clock)
%I	hour (12-hour clock)
%j	day of the year
%m	month (numeric)
%M	minute
%p	AM/PM
%S	second
%V	week number (Sunday as first day of week)
%w	day of the week (numeric)
%W	week number (Monday as first day of week)
%x	local date
%X	local time

%y   year number, without century
%Y   year number, including century
%Z   time zone name
%%   %

The description of standard functions here has been necessarily brief, with the intention of introducing the facilities that are provided in this way. Readers wishing to make use of particular functions may find it useful to refer to the extended documentation of the functions that is usually available locally, often in online media.

5.5   Exercises

1. Write the following macros:

```
int isodd(int n)
      /* delivers TRUE if n is odd otherwise FALSE */

int iseven(int n)
      /* delivers TRUE if n is even otherwise FALSE */

int isinorder(int n1, int n2, int n3)
      /* delivers TRUE if arguments are in
         increasing size */
```

2. Write a program that computes the word length distribution for the words in a specified file.

   (a) Your program should accept a file name that is supplied as an argument on the command line.

   (b) If no filename is supplied on the command line then your program should prompt for a file name.

   (c) You may assume that the file contains some document of written text.

   (d) You may assume that words only contain alphabetic characters.

   (e) Your output should be of the form:

```
               3 words with 1 character
               7 words with 2 characters
               . . .
```

3. Adapt your solution to Exercise 2 above so that it can produce output in any one of three different languages. The language should be selected prior to compilation, and only the relevant code for the chosen language should be compiled.

4. A simple mechanism for encrypting textual data is to replace every alphabetic character with the letter that occurs some fixed distance from it in the alphabet. The distance is determined by a *key* value. Non-alphabetic characters are not encrypted. Thus:

Zebra!
encrypted with a key of 2 becomes:
Bgdtc!
or encrypted with a key of -1 becomes:
Ydaqz!

Write a program that firstly reads the encryption key and then reads the contents of a named text file, generating an output file which contains the encrypted version of the original text.

Write a complementary program to decipher an encrypted file.

5. Write a function that determines whether a given name is a valid identifier for a data item in C. Remember, the rules for forming C identifiers are:

(a) It must start with either a letter or an underscore.

(b) It must contain only alphabetic, numeric or underscore characters.

(c) It cannot be a C reserved word.

6. Write a program that 'indents' another program by following three simple rules:

(a) Ignore any existing indentation.

(b) If the first printing character on the line is an open curly bracket increase the indent level by three spaces.

(c) If the first printing character on the line is a close curly bracket decrease the indent level by three spaces.

7. Write a program that reads a text file and justifies its contents, using both right- and left-justification. The justified text should be written to an output file. The line length of the output file should be supplied as data to the program. Your program should not split words between lines and should, as far as possible, evenly space the words on the output line. Paragraphs will be separated in the input file by a blank line.

8. Write a pair of macros to be used to read (write) an array, whose elements can be of any data type, from (to) a file in binary form. Each macro will take four parameters:

   - the file to be read (written) i.e. a FILE *;
   - the array;
   - the data type of the array;
   - the number of elements in the array.

9. A file contains data representing the bank balances of a group of small businesses that all trade with each other. The details of each account are given in a fixed format on a separate line and consist of an account name, which is extended with spaces to occupy 20 characters, followed by the current balance which occupies 10 characters. Write a program that allows two types of transaction on the data in the file, namely:

   (a) **Deposit** to allow money to be deposited in a named account. The balance of the specified account should be updated by the amount specified, e.g.:

       Deposit PhotoLabs 101.50

   (b) **Transfer** to facilitate the transfer of monies between two accounts. This requires the names of the accounts to be debited and credited and the amount to be specified respectively, e.g.:

       Transfer PhotoLabs Print-a-Pic 40.75

   No account should be allowed to become overdrawn, thus the program should check there are sufficient funds in the account being debited to cover the transfer before the balances are updated.

Chapter 6

Structures

6.1 Defining data structures

In Chapter 3, we saw that it is possible in C to declare and use an array of elements, each of which is of a defined type. A **structure** is a more general form of multiple data type, in which the individual elements may be of different types.

We can define the **form** of a structure by giving it a name, and describing the elements of which it is composed. Thus, for example:

```
struct class_record{int size;float average_mark;
                            int pass_mark,number_pass;};
```

This declaration introduces a structure to which is given the **structure tag class_record**, and which comprises four **members**: the variables `size`, `average_mark`, `pass_mark` and `number_pass`, each of which has a defined type.

The definition of a structure in this way does not in itself declare any new variables; rather, the structure declaration describes the kind of object that will be referred to when we use the structure tag `class_record`. To declare a variable of this type, we need a further declaration:

```
struct class_record year1,year2,year3;
```

This declaration introduces three variables, each of which is of the **type** defined by the earlier declaration of the structure `class_record`; that is, each of `year1`, `year2` and `year3` is a multiple data object comprising four separately identified members. We refer to these members using the '.' operator; for example:

151

```
year1.average_mark
```

refers to the second identified member of the structure variable `year1`. The type of `year1.average_mark` is defined by the declaration of the structure `class_record`, i.e. `float`, and `year1.average_mark` behaves like any other variable of type `float`.

We can, if we choose, combine the structure type declaration with the declaration of variables of the new type:

```
struct lib_record{char name[21];int num_books_out;
                                 float fine_due;}jones;
```

This defines the structure type `lib_record`, and declares a variable `jones` of this type. Notice that a member of a structure may be an array; we would refer to an element of this array member of `jones` thus:

```
jones.name[0]   /* the first character of the
                   member 'name' in 'jones' */
```

If we intend to declare all the variables of a particular structure in a single declaration, then there is no need to introduce a structure tag to identify the type of the structure.

```
struct {char term;char *sentence;int length;}text,text1;
```

This declaration introduces two variables, `text` and `text1`, whose type is the anonymous structure shown. Here, one of the members of the structure is a pointer, with member-name `sentence` and type `char *`. To refer to the character pointed to by `sentence`, we would write, for example:

```
*text.sentence
```

Generalizing the above, structure declarations take the form:

```
struct < structure tag > {< member list >} < variable list >;
```

where either the < *structure tag* > or the < *variable list* > may be omitted (in the case of a structure type declaration), or the < *member list* > may be omitted (when declaring variables of a previously defined structure type).

Figure 6.1 illustrates the use of a structure declaration in a simple program. Here we have defined a structure with the tag `stock_item` to describe a composite object including an array of characters and three associated numeric values. In the `main()` function, a variable `hammer` is declared to be of this type, and the library function `strcpy()` (described in Section 5.4) is used to initialize the `name` member of this variable by copying the string `"hammer"` into it. After initializing the other members of `hammer`,

```
/* This program illustrates the definition of a structure
 * type and the referencing of a structure member. */
#include <stdio.h>
#include <string.h>
struct stock_item{ char name[21]; float cost;
                                  int number,min_level;};

/*-------------------------------------------------------*/

float value_of(struct stock_item item)
{
  float value = item.number*item.cost;
  return value;
}

/*-------------------------------------------------------*/
main()
{
  struct stock_item hammer;
  strcpy(hammer.name,"hammer");
  hammer.cost = 2.15;
  hammer.number = 10;
  hammer.min_level = 25;
  printf("value of hammers in stock=%f\n",value_of(hammer));
}
```

Figure 6.1   Example of the use of a structure

the function **value_of**() is called to calculate the value of the stock item represented by this structure variable. Notice that this function has a structure as its parameter; the type of the parameter, specified in the function declaration, is written as **struct stock_item**, and is given the formal parameter-name **item**.

Arrays of structures

The most common use of structured data types is to define **table** structures, and similar information structures in which we require to declare a number of records, each being a composite of several values. In these cases we must declare an **array** of structures. For example, suppose we have defined a structure type with the structure tag **stock_item**, as in Figure 6.1:

```
struct stock_item{char name[21];float cost;
                            int number,min_level;};
```

Then we can declare an array of variables of this type in just the same way as we declare arrays of any other type:

```
struct stock_item stock_list[100];
```

This declares an array of 100 records of this structure, given the array-name **stock_list**. Notice again that the name of the type used in this declaration is written as **struct stock_item**.

A single element of the array is referenced by subscripting the array-name, in the usual way:

```
stock_list[10]; /* refers to a single stock_item */
```

Then we can refer to a member of this element by applying the '.' operator, as before:

```
stock_list[10].cost;    /* the 'cost' member of
                          stock_list[10] */

stock_list[10].name[0]; /* the first character of the
                          'name' of stock_list[10] */
```

Figure 6.2 is a more substantial program involving the use of an array of structures. The structure type used is again **stock_item**, but in this case we have declared not a fixed-size array, but a variable **stock_record** which is a **pointer** to structures of this type. The program assumes that the actual stock items are contained in a **file** with the name **stock_file**, and the first action of **main()** is to open this file for reading, assigning the file-pointer returned to the variable **stock_file_ptr**. The first item in the file is an integer value, defining the number of records stored, and this value is read and assigned to **num_records** by the first call of **fscanf()**.

main() proceeds to allocate space in which to store the array of stock items by a call of **malloc()**. To determine how much space is needed, the **sizeof** operator is applied to the structure type **struct stock_item**, and the value obtained is multiplied by the number of records. The call of **malloc()** returns a pointer to an area of memory large enough to store this set of records, which is assigned to the structure-pointer **stock_record** declared at the start of the program. Now the function **input_stock()** is used to read successive stock items from the file into the area referenced by this

```
/* A program to calculate the value of items held in stock.
 * The stock position is read from the file 'stock_file'.
 * This file contains the number of stock lines.
 * For each stock line an entry giving name, cost, number
 * in stock and the minimum level of stock to be held.
   A sample 'stock_file'
3
hammer 2.15 15 25
pliers 1.75 47 25
mallet 2.75 23 10
 */

#include <stdio.h>
#include <ctype.h>
#include <stdlib.h>

struct stock_item{ char name[21]; float cost;
                                   int number,min_level;};

struct stock_item *stock_record;
FILE *stock_file_ptr;
int num_records;

float value_stock(int, struct stock_item *);
void input_stock(int, struct stock_item *, FILE *);
float value_of(struct stock_item);

/*----------------------------------------------------------*/

float value_stock(int num, struct stock_item *stock)
{
   float total = 0.0;
   int i;

   for (i=0; i<num; i++)
   {
      total += value_of(stock[i]);
   }
   return total;
}

/*----------------------------------------------------------*/
```

```
main()
{
   int i; float value;

   if ((stock_file_ptr = fopen("stock_file","r"))==NULL)
   {
      printf("unable to open 'stock_file' for reading\n");
      exit(1);
   }

   fscanf(stock_file_ptr,"%d",&num_records);
   if (num_records==0)
   {
      printf("stock_file is empty!\n"); exit(2);
   }

   stock_record =
         malloc(sizeof(struct stock_item)*num_records);

   if (stock_record == 0)
   {
      printf("not enough memory to house stock_file\n");
      exit(3);
   }

   input_stock(num_records,stock_record,stock_file_ptr);

   fclose(stock_file_ptr);
   value = value_stock(num_records,stock_record);
   printf("total stock value is %f pounds\n",value);
}
/*-----------------------------------------------------------*/

float value_of(struct stock_item item)
{
   float value = item.number*item.cost;

   return value;
}

/*-----------------------------------------------------------*/
```

```
void input_stock(int num, struct stock_item *stock,
                                        FILE *in_file)
{
    int i;

    for (i=0; i<num; i++)
    {
        fscanf(in_file,"%s %f %d %d\n",stock[i].name,
        &stock[i].cost, &stock[i].number,&stock[i].min_level);
    }
}
```

Figure 6.2   Example of the use of an array of structures

pointer. The function **value_stock()** is used to calculate the total stock value, using in turn the function **value_of()** to obtain the value of a single stock item. Notice that these functions, declared following **main()**, were introduced by means of function prototypes at the start of the program.

It may be found helpful to examine the storage of these structures using our debugging system. Figure 6.3 shows a line-numbered listing of the relevant program section.

If we stop the program after the records have been read into memory, we can examine the way they have been stored:

> *? show &stock.record*
> *0x7488*

(The pointer-variable **stock_record** is located at address *7488* (hexadecimal). Of course, all such addresses will be implementation-specific.)

> *? show stock.record*
> *0x868c*

(The space allocated to store the array of stock items starts at address *868c*.)

> *? show stock.record[0]*
> *0x868c   struct{*
> *   name = "hammer";*

```
61:    stock_record =
62             malloc(sizeof(struct stock_item)*num_records);
63:
64:    if (stock_record == 0)
65:    {
66:        printf("not enough memory to house stock_file\n");
67:    }
68:
69:    input_stock(num_records,stock_record,stock_file_ptr);
70:
71:    fclose(stock_file_ptr);
72:    value = value_stock(num_records,stock_record);
73:    printf("total stock value is %f pounds\n",value);
74: }
75:
```

Figure 6.3   A line-numbered listing of part of the program of Figure 6.2

```
            cost = 2.15;
            number = 15;
            min_level = 25;
        }
? next
0x86ac    struct{
            name = "pliers";
            cost = 1.75;
            number = 47;
            min_level = 25;
        }
? next
0x86cc    struct{
            name = "mallet";
            cost = 2.75;
            number = 23;
            min_level = 10;
        }
?
```

Figure 6.4 shows a pictorial representation of the memory organization described by this sequence.

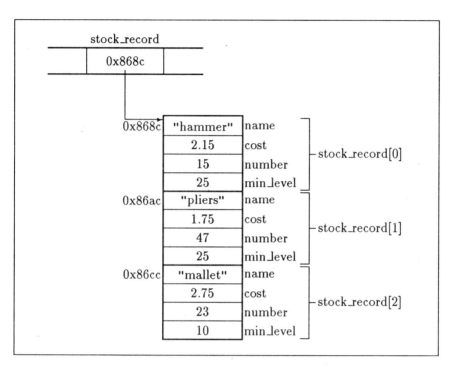

Figure 6.4   Memory allocation for the program of Figure 6.2

The program of Figure 6.2 used the character input function `fscanf()` to read the records from the stock file. Figure 6.5 includes two functions, `read_bin()` and `write_bin()`, that could have been used with this program had it been necessary to use binary storage for the records.

Pointers to structures

We often wish to reference structures using pointers. This is particularly so when a non-local structure is referenced from within a function. If the structure is passed to the function as a parameter, then the whole structure is copied; more usually, therefore, only the address of the structure is passed as a pointer-parameter.

To reference a structure via its pointer, the pointer is first dereferenced using the '*' operator; we may then apply the '.' operator to reference a

```
void read_bin(char *name, struct stock_item *stock)
{
   FILE *b_in;
   int num;

   if ( (b_in = fopen(name,"r"))==NULL)
   {
      printf("unable to open '%s' for reading\n",name);
      exit(7);
   }

   if (fread(&num,sizeof(int),1,b_in) != 1)
   {
      printf("Error:- when reading from %s\n",name);
      exit(8);
   }

   if (fread(stock,sizeof(struct stock_item),num,b_in)!=num)
   {
      printf("Error:- when reading from %s\n",name);
      exit(9);
   }

   fclose(b_in);
}

/*-------------------------------------------------------------*/

void write_bin(char *name, struct stock_item *stock,int num)
{
   FILE *b_out;

   if ( (b_out = fopen(name,"w"))==NULL)
   {
      printf("unable to open '%s' for writing\n",name);
      exit(4);
   }
```

```
    if (fwrite(&num,sizeof(int),1,b_out) != 1)
    {
        printf("Error:- when writing to %s\n",name);
        exit(5);
    }

    if (fwrite(stock,
                sizeof(struct stock_item),num,b_out) != num)
    {
        printf("Error encountered when writing to %s\n",name);
        exit(6);
    }

    fclose(b_out);
}
```

Figure 6.5   Functions for binary transput of structures

member of the structure. In general:

$$(* < pointer\ to\ structure >) . < member\ name >$$

Using the structure `stock_item` declared in Figures 6.1 and 6.2, we could declare a pointer to a structure of this type thus:

`struct stock_item *item_ptr;`

Then we can refer to the `cost` member of the structure referred to by the expression:

`(*item_ptr).cost`

Note again the need to bracket the dereferencing expression because of the higher priority of the '.' operator.

This kind of combination is so common that C has a special operator, '->', which enables direct access to a member of a structure referenced via a pointer. Thus the expression above could also be written more conveniently as:

`item_ptr->cost`

In Figure 6.6, we have rewritten the program of Figure 6.1 so that the function value_of() takes a parameter that is a pointer to the structure rather than the structure itself.

Notice also that, in Figure 6.6, the structure variable hammer is initialized with a composite assignment, in the same way as we can perform a multiple assignment to an array.

```c
/* This program illustrates the definition of a structure
 * type and the referencing of a structure member via a
 * pointer. */
#include <stdio.h>

struct stock_item{ char name[20]; float cost;
                                   int number,min_level;};

/*------------------------------------------------------------*/

float value_of(struct stock_item *item_ptr)
{
    float value = item_ptr->number*item_ptr->cost;
    return value;
}

/*------------------------------------------------------------*/

main()
{
    struct stock_item hammer = {"hammer", 2.15, 10, 25};
    printf("value of hammers in stock=%f\n",
                                    value_of(&hammer));
}
```

Figure 6.6   Structures and pointers

6.2   Type definitions

Structures provide a way in which we can define new data types to describe the kinds of information required in our programs. If we wish, we can give a new name to a type thus defined, or indeed to any other type. We do this by means of a **typedef** declaration, for which the general form is:

typedef < *data type* >< *alternative name* >

A declaration of this kind defines < *alternative name* > to be a synonym for the already defined type name (or structure description) < *data type* >. For example:

```
typedef float REAL;    /* defines REAL to be a
                          synonym for type float */
```

We can in fact, if we wish, define more than one alternative name in a single **typedef** declaration, or we can also define a name for a pointer to the type; thus:

```
typedef float REAL,*REFREAL;
```

defines **REAL** to be an alternative name for **float**, and **REFREAL** to be a name for the pointer type **float***.

The rules for constructing new type names are the same as for other identifiers, although by convention they usually contain at least one uppercase character. We can use new type names, as we do variable identifiers, to make our programs easier to read and understand. Most often, this facility will be used to define shorter and clearer names for structured types:

```
typedef struct complex{REAL re,im;} COMPLEX;
```

Here we have defined the name **COMPLEX** which we can now use instead of the cumbersome form **struct complex**. Also:

```
typedef struct{char name [21];int age;
               float height,weight;} Description;
```

Description is now the name given to the (otherwise anonymous) structured type described here.

Figure 6.7 uses **typedef** declarations in a program to perform arithmetic on complex numbers. The advantages here are clarity and brevity; once the original **typedef** declaration has been made, the name **COMPLEX** is used throughout to stand for a data structure comprising two **REAL** (i.e. **float**) type members.

Enumeration data types

The definition of a structure, with or without a name declared using **typedef**, is one way of introducing a new data type for use in a program. Another kind of user-defined data type is an **enumeration type**. An enumeration type is specified by itemizing all the values of this type. For example:

```
/* This program illustrates the use of 'typedef' in
 * implementing a small library of complex arithmetic
 * functions.
 */
#include <stdio.h>

typedef float REAL;
typedef struct {REAL re, im;} COMPLEX;

/*----------------------------------------------------------*/

void print_complex(COMPLEX c)
{
   printf("%f %+fi",c.re,c.im);
}

/*----------------------------------------------------------*/

void read_complex(COMPLEX *c_ptr)
{
   scanf("%f %f",&c_ptr->re,&c_ptr->im);
}

/*----------------------------------------------------------*/

COMPLEX add_complex(COMPLEX c1, COMPLEX c2)
{
   COMPLEX temp;

   temp.re = c1.re + c2.re;
   temp.im = c1.im + c2.im;

   return temp;
}

/*----------------------------------------------------------*/
```

```
COMPLEX sub_complex(COMPLEX c1, COMPLEX c2)
{
    COMPLEX temp;

    temp.re = c1.re - c2.re;
    temp.im = c1.im - c2.im;

    return temp;
}

/*--------------------------------------------------------*/

main()
{
    COMPLEX x,y,sum,dif;

    printf("Input complex x\n");
    read_complex(&x);
    printf("\nInput complex y\n");
    read_complex(&y);

    sum = add_complex(x,y);

    dif = sub_complex(x,y);

    printf("\nThe sum of x & y is ");
    print_complex(sum);
    printf("\nThe difference of x & y is ");
    print_complex(dif);
}
```

Figure 6.7 Example to illustrate the use of `typedef`

```
enum cities{London,Birmingham,Liverpool,Manchester,
          Glasgow,Edinburgh,Leeds,Newcastle,Cardiff};
```

This declaration introduces a new enumeration type that is given the tag cities. The names London, Birmingham,...etc., which are enumerated in the declaration, form a complete *ordered* set of symbolic constants that are used to represent the values of this type. The *actual* values implied when these names are used are 0,1,2... for London, Birmingham, Liverpool... respectively. We can, if we wish, associate different values with the symbolic names in the enumeration:

```
enum chinese_years{rabbit=1987,dragon,snake,horse,goat,
          monkey,rooster,dog,pig,rat,ox,tiger};
```

In this case, the symbolic constant rabbit is equivalent to the number 1987; dragon=1988, snake=1989, and so on. Also, values need not only be simple integers (although they must be of one of the integer-valued types):

```
enum punctuation{comma=',',period='.',semicolon=';',
          hyphen='-',question='?',exclamation='!'};
```

These kinds of declaration can be used simply to define a set of symbolic constants in a convenient way. However, we can also, if we wish, declare variables that are defined to be of an enumeration type; the declaration:

```
enum chinese_years thisyear;
```

declares a variable thisyear, whose type is defined to be the enumeration type chinese_years, defined earlier. The implication of this declaration is that the only valid values of the variable thisyear are the constants rabbit, dragon, snake,...etc., itemized in the enumeration of chinese_years; however, not all compilers will check the validity of assignments to enum variables.

Figure 6.8 illustrates the use of enumeration data types in a program to perform currency conversion. The enumeration type country defines a set of symbolic constants, representing the countries for which currency conversion can be performed. The function exchange() takes as its second parameter a variable, code, which is of the type enum country. This parameter is used in a switch statement to select the appropriate conversion to be used.

Note that we cannot directly read the symbolic value of an enum variable. The program of Figure 6.8 reads a string, which might be 'Italy', assigning it to the character array nation. The function translate() is used to identify the value of type enum country corresponding to this string.

```
/* This program illustrates the use of enumeration data
 * types by way of a simple currency exchange program. */
#include <stdio.h>
#include <string.h>


enum country {France,Germany,Italy,Japan,
                            USA,NOTLISTED = -1};

enum country translate(char *);
void exchange(int,enum country);

/*-----------------------------------------------------------*/


void exchange(int pounds, enum country code)
{
   char currency [50];
   float rate;

   switch(code)
   {
      case France: rate = 10.32;
         strcpy(currency,"french francs");
         break;
      case Germany: rate = 3.038;
         strcpy(currency,"marks");
         break;
      case Italy: rate = 2202;
         strcpy(currency,"lire");
         break;
      case Japan: rate = 218.8;
         strcpy(currency,"yen");
         break;
      case USA: rate = 1.550;
         strcpy(currency,"dollars");
         break;
   }
   printf("\n%-d pounds gives %f %s\n",
                    pounds,pounds*rate,currency);
}

/*-----------------------------------------------------------*/
```

```
enum country translate(char *name)
{
   if (strcmp(name,"France")==0)
      return France;
   else if (strcmp(name,"Germany")==0)
      return Germany ;
   else if (strcmp(name,"Italy")==0)
      return Italy;
   else if (strcmp(name,"Japan")==0)
      return Japan;
   else if (strcmp(name,"USA")==0)
      return USA;
   return NOTLISTED;
}

/*-------------------------------------------------------*/

main()
{
   char nation[51];
   int amount;
   enum country country_code;

   printf("Type how much sterling you want exchanged\n");
   printf("Then type the country whose currency you want");
   printf("\nFrance/Germany/Italy/Japan/USA\n");
   printf("eg. 45 France\n");

   scanf("%d %50s",&amount,nation);

   country_code = translate(nation);

   if (country_code != NOTLISTED)
      exchange(amount,country_code);
   else
      printf("We do not stock currency for %s\n",nation);
}
```

Figure 6.8   Example of the use of enumeration data types

6.3 Linked data structures

One of the most useful applications of structured data types is to define organizations of data in which distinct items are linked together using pointers. The simplest general form of linked structure is a **list**. We often visualize a list as a set of cells, each of which comprises a value (which may be a simple integer, or something more complex), and a pointer to a succeeding cell (Figure 6.9). The last item in the list is indicated by a special pointer value, such as 0 (NULL).

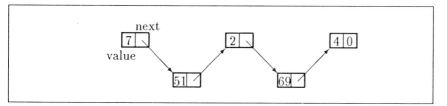

Figure 6.9   A simple list of integers

We can declare a cell of the type required to create a list such as the one shown in Figure 6.9, using the declaration:

```
typedef struct cell{int value;struct cell *next;} CELL;
```

This declares a structure with tag **cell**, the members of which are a **value** of type **int**, and a **pointer** (**next**) to a cell of similar structure. Note the **recursive** nature of the definition, characteristic of this kind of structure; the structure declaration includes a member which is a pointer to the same kind of structure.

In this case, we have used a **typedef** declaration to define the name CELL for a structure of this type. Now we can declare, for example, pointers to cells of this type:

```
CELL *start, *end, *current;
```

Pointers of this kind usually play an important part in programs involving manipulations of lists. We use them to indicate positions within the composite list structure, as illustrated in Figure 6.10, for example.

One of the important characteristics of list structures is that they are inherently extensible; extra cells can be added on at the end of the list, or inserted in the middle, by suitable assignments of pointers. They are therefore very useful when we wish to deal with sets of information of unknown size, especially when it is necessary both to add new information (cells) and to remove information no longer needed.

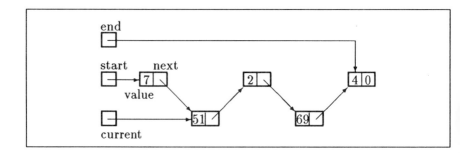

Figure 6.10   Pointers to cells in a list

A linked list example

To explore these ideas further we will examine a fairly substantial program involving the use of linked list structures to maintain a record of visitors to some establishment. The information recorded for each visitor comprises the visitor's name and times of arrival and departure. This set of values constitutes the 'cells' in our list structures. We need to add new cells to a list when a new visitor arrives, and to locate a cell in the list when the visitor departs. In addition, we wish to maintain separate records of visitors currently present and of those who have departed, so we also need to be able to remove a cell from a list.

Figure 6.11 shows the main part of the program, including the global declarations and function prototypes. The structure:

```
struct visitor{char name [21];TIME arrive,depart;
                        struct visitor *next;}
```

is to be used for the cells in the list; notice again the characteristic recursive form of this definition, including a pointer to a **struct visitor** within itself. **TIME** has been defined to be synonymous with **long**, for purely documentary purposes. The type name **VISITOR** has been declared to represent a type of this structure, and the name **VISITOR_PTR** represents a type that is a pointer to **struct visitor**. This allows two lists to be started, by the declarations:

```
VISITOR_PTR visitors_here = NULL,visitors_left = NULL;
```

At this point, of course, no actual lists exist; that is, no space has been allocated in which to store any visitor records. What we have so far are two pointers, initialized to null values, that are subsequently used

```
/* This program is an example of the use of 'lists'.
 * A 'visitors book' is managed, arrivals and departures are
 * noted. The printing of those who are present or those
 * who have left is allowed. */

#include <stdio.h>
#include <stdlib.h>
#include <time.h>
#include <ctype.h>
#define BOOL int
#define TRUE 1
#define FALSE 0

typedef long TIME;
typedef struct visitor{char name[21]; TIME arrive, depart;
              struct visitor *next;} VISITOR, *VISITOR_PTR;

/* Function prototypes:- */
void deal_with_arrival(void), deal_with_departure(void),
      print_visitors_here(void), print_visitors_left(void);
VISITOR_PTR create_visitor(void);
void add_to_list(VISITOR_PTR, VISITOR_PTR *);
VISITOR_PTR find_and_unhook(char *, VISITOR_PTR *);

VISITOR_PTR visitors_here = NULL, visitors_left = NULL;

/*-----------------------------------------------------------*/

main()
{
   char event;

   while(TRUE)
   {
      printf("\nInput the next command\n");
      printf("Type initial char of any of the following");
      printf("\n arrive, depart, here_record,"
                                   " left_record, quit\n");
      printf("Followed by <Return>\n");
      scanf(" %c",&event); event = tolower(event);
```

```
        switch(event)
        {
            case 'a': deal_with_arrival();
                      break;
            case 'd': deal_with_departure();
                      break;
            case 'h': print_visitors_here();
                      break;
            case 'l': print_visitors_left();
                      break;
            case 'q': exit(0); break;
            default:  printf("\n*Invalid! %c typed*\n",event);
        }
    }
}
```

Figure 6.11   Main part of the visitors' book program

to point to the start of the two lists: one to record the visitors currently present, the other to record those who have left. The function `main()` provides an outline of the actions that can be carried out by the program. In response to a single-character command input, the program will invoke one of four functions, the function prototypes of which appear among the declarations in Figure 6.11: `deal_with_arrival()`, which will create a new visitor record, adding it to the list pointed to by `visitors_here`; `deal_with_departure()`, which takes a record from the `visitors_here` list and adds it to the `visitors_left` list; and two functions to print out the values of the two lists. These, and the other functions that they make use of, are described in turn below.

Adding an element to a list

Figure 6.12 continues the visitors' book program, with the declaration of the function `deal_with_arrival()` and of two functions that it calls in turn.

The first action of `deal_with_arrival()` is to call `create_visitor()` to create a new visitor record. Within the latter function, `malloc()` is used to allocate memory space for a structure of the size of `VISITOR`; the variable `new` (of type `VISITOR_PTR`) points to this. Details of the new arrival are

```
void deal_with_arrival()
{
   VISITOR_PTR arrival;

   arrival = create_visitor();

   add_to_list(arrival,&visitors_here);
}

/*----------------------------------------------------------*/

VISITOR_PTR create_visitor(void)
{
   VISITOR_PTR new;

   new = malloc( sizeof(VISITOR) );

   if (new==0)
   {
      printf("\n*** Run out of memory - Sorry!\n");
      exit(1);
   }

   printf("Hello & welcome\nWhat is your name?\n");
   scanf("%20s",new->name);
   /* set arrival time */
   new->arrive = time( (TIME*) 0);

   return new;
}

/*----------------------------------------------------------*/

void add_to_list(VISITOR_PTR new, VISITOR_PTR *listptr)
{
   /* Link the new arrival into the visitors list. */
   new->next = *listptr;
   *listptr = new;
}
```

Figure 6.12   Adding an element to a list

then read and assigned to members of the structure pointed to (recall that
new->name will refer to the name member of the structure pointed to by
new). The library function time() is used to obtain the current time; as
the parameter of this is not being used, it is supplied as a NULL pointer
to TIME.

The call of create_visitor() returns a pointer (type VISITOR_PTR) to
the new structure created, which is assigned to the pointer variable arrival
in deal_with_arrival(). At this point it may be helpful to visualize the
state of the structures in use with the help of a pictorial representation.
Suppose that just two visitors, named Dan and Zoe, had arrived previously;
then the visitors_here list may be visualized as shown in Figure 6.13(a).
The pointer visitors_here contains the address of the first record in the
list, containing the details for Dan, and this in turn points to the record
for Zoe. After calling create_visitor(), a new record has been created
for a visitor named Mia; the address of this record is contained in arrival
(Figure 6.13(b)).

The final step in deal_with_arrival() is to add this new record to
the visitor_here list. It does so by calling the function add_to_list()
with the pointer variable arrival (the address of the new record) and
the *address* of the list pointer visitors_here as its actual parameters.
The new record is added at the *head* of the list (Figure 6.13(c)). This
is done, in the function add_to_list(), by first assigning to the member
next of the new structure (i.e. Mia's record) the previous value contained
in the list pointer parameter (i.e. the address of Dan's record). This has
the effect of joining the list comprising the records for Dan and Zoe on
to the 'tail' of Mia's record. The new list thus formed commences with
the record for Mia, so the address of this record (new, in add_to_list())
is assigned to the pointer variable listptr, i.e. to the actual parameter
variable visitors_here. It is because we needed to change the value of
the pointer variable visitors_here that we had to pass its *address* as the
parameter to add_to_list(). The sequence of assignments is represented
pictorially in Figure 6.14.

Finding and unlinking an element

When a visitor departs, the procedure followed is represented in the function deal_with_departure() (Figure 6.15). Suppose that the person leaving is Dan. The action of the function is to detach the record for Dan
from the visitors_here list, using the function find_and_unhook() to
do so, and to assign the address of this record to the pointer variable
departee. These effects are illustrated in Figure 6.16. After this is done,
deal_with_departure() updates the record for Dan by adding his depar-

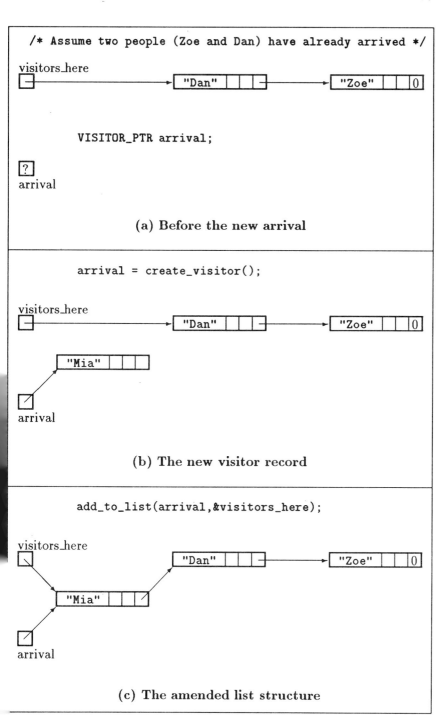

```
/* Assume two people (Zoe and Dan) have already arrived */
```

visitors_here

"Dan"   "Zoe" 0

```
VISITOR_PTR arrival;
```

?
arrival

(a) Before the new arrival

```
arrival = create_visitor();
```

visitors_here

"Dan"   "Zoe" 0

"Mia"

arrival

(b) The new visitor record

```
add_to_list(arrival,&visitors_here);
```

visitors_here

"Dan"   "Zoe" 0

"Mia"

arrival

(c) The amended list structure

Figure 6.13 Adding a new record to the visitors_here list

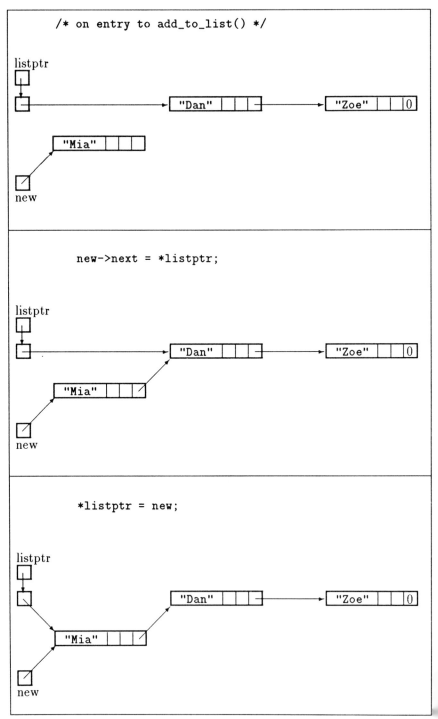

Figure 6.14 Sequence of assignments in add_to_list

```
void deal_with_departure(void)
{
   char leavers_name[21];
   VISITOR_PTR departee;

   printf("\nWhat is your name?\n");
   scanf("%20s",leavers_name);
   departee = find_and_unhook(leavers_name, &visitors_here);
   if (departee == NULL)
      printf("\nNo record of '%s' arriving\n",leavers_name);
   else
   {
      /* set departure time */
      departee->depart = time( (TIME*) 0);
      add_to_list(departee, &visitors_left);
   }
}

/*---------------------------------------------------------*/

VISITOR_PTR find_and_unhook(char * name_of_leaver,
                                   VISITOR_PTR *listptr)
{
   BOOL found = FALSE;
   VISITOR_PTR link = *listptr;

   while (link!=NULL && !found)
   {
      if (strcmp(name_of_leaver, link->name)==0)
      {
         found = TRUE;
         /* unhook from list */
         *listptr = link->next;
      }
      else
      {
         listptr = &link->next;
         link = link->next;
      }
   }
   return link;
}
```

Figure 6.15   The visitors' book program continued

ture time, and then appends the record to the `visitors_left` list (usin
the same function, `add_to_list()`, as was used to add a new arrival to th
`visitors_here` list).

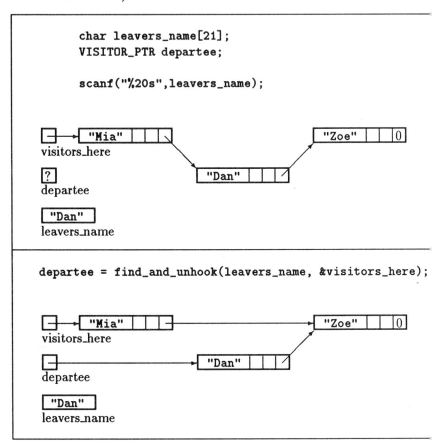

Figure 6.16 Unlink an element from a list (from `deal_with_departure()`)

The steps involved in `find_and_unhook()` are examined more closel
in Figure 6.17. At the start of the function, the formal parameter `listpt`
contains the address of the list pointer `visitors_here`, which in turn point
to the `visitors_here` list. The local variable `link` is of type `VISITOR_PTF`
i.e. a pointer to the list cell structure, and the assignment:

```
link = *listptr;
```

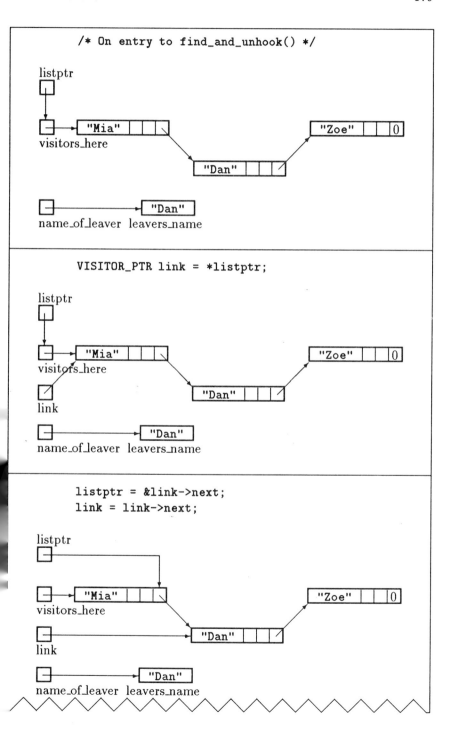

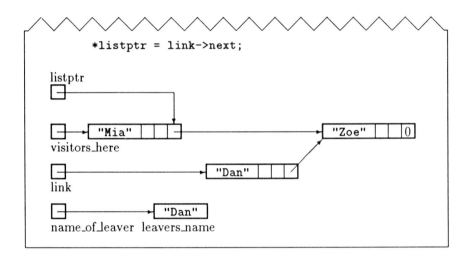

Figure 6.17   Looking at find_and_unhook()

assigns to this pointer the contents of the location pointed to by `listptr`, i.e. the address of the first cell in the list.

The function proceeds to compare the `name_of_leaver` ("Dan") with the `name` member of the cell pointed to by `link` ("Mia"). When the comparison fails, the `link` pointer is advanced to point to the successor of "Mia" in the list (`link->next`). Before this assignment, however, `listptr` is assigned to point to the `next` member of Mia's record, i.e. to its list pointer member. The reason for this becomes apparent when the next comparison is made. Now, the `name_of_leaver`, "Dan", matches the `name` member of the cell pointed to by `link`. The variable `link` points correctly to the cell that must be returned, so it only remains to detach this from the `visitors_here` list. This is achieved by the single assignment:

```
*listptr = link->next;
```

The right-hand side of this assignment specifies the `next` member of the cell pointed to by `link`. This is the `next` member of the cell for Dan, i.e. the address of "Zoe". This address is assigned to the location *pointed to* by `listptr` (`*listptr`). As `listptr` currently points to the `next` member of the cell for Mia, it is this variable which is altered, to give the result shown in the final stage of Figure 6.17. Note also that, had the matching element been the first one in the list, the effect of an assignment to `*listptr` would have been to update the head-of-list pointer variable, `visitors_here`; it

```
void print_visitors_here(void)
{
   VISITOR_PTR link;

   link = visitors_here;

   if (link==NULL)
       printf("No visitors here at present\n");
   else printf("The visitors here are:\n");

   while (link != NULL)
   {
       printf("%s arrived %s",link->name,
                                      ctime(&link->arrive));
       /* move onto the next */
       link = link->next;
   }
}

/*--------------------------------------------------------*/

void print_visitors_left(void)
{
   VISITOR_PTR link;

   link = visitors_left;

   if (link==NULL)
       printf("No visitors left so far\n");
   else printf("The visitors which have left are:\n");

   while (link != NULL)
   {
       printf("%s arrived %s",link->name,
                                      ctime(&link->arrive));
       printf("Left %s",ctime(&link->depart));
       /* move onto the next */
       link = link->next;
   }
}
```

Figure 6.18   Printing elements of the list

is for this reason that `listptr` must be a *pointer* to a VISITOR_PTR, i.e. a pointer to a pointer to a list cell.

The remaining functions of the visitors' book program are those to print out the contents of the lists, shown as Figure 6.18. These are straightforward; in each case the **VISITOR_PTR link** is used to step along the list, element-by-element. The function `ctime()` is used to convert the stored time of arrival or departure, as obtained by the `time()` function, into a printable string.

Trees

Another widely-used form of linked data structure is a **tree**. A tree is a generalization of a list structure, in that each cell (or **node** of the tree, as it is usually called) can include pointers to a number of other cells. The simplest case is that in which each node has two successors, to create a **binary tree** (Figure 6.19).

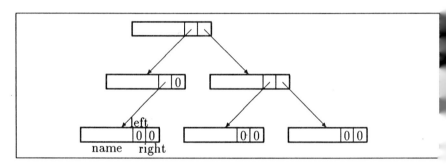

Figure 6.19   A binary tree

We can declare a structure appropriate for the nodes of this type thus:

```
typedef struct node {char name [26];
                     struct node *left,*right;} NODE;
```

As with list structures, we are likely to make use of pointer variables to indicate positions within the tree structure, such as its starting node (or **root**), or the start of a particular sub-tree:

```
NODE *root,*sub_tree;
```

One of the important applications of binary tree structures is to provide a simple and efficient framework for storing information in a defined order

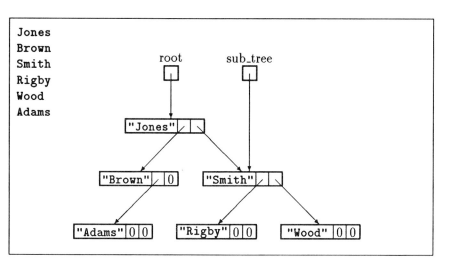

Figure 6.20   Names in alphabetical order on a tree

Figure 6.20 illustrates this, for the case in which the information stored consists of names that are required to be placed in alphabetical order. It may not be immediately clear that the structure of Figure 6.20 has achieved this. However, if we examine the root node "Jones", we will see that all those names stored on the *right* branch of this node (i.e. the sub-tree whose root is "Smith") *follow* "Jones" in alphabetical order. Likewise, those stored on the *left* branch of "Jones" precede it alphabetically. Hence, to find a name in the structure, we have a simple algorithm:

1. Compare the name to be found with that of the root node.

2. If they are different, examine either the left or right sub-tree (depending on whether the name to be found precedes or follows that of the root node).

3. Repeat from step 1 until the name is found, or the end of a branch is reached.

Not only is this method simple, it is also efficient. It is easy to see from Figure 6.20 that at most three comparisons have to be made in order to locate any name in the structure. By contrast, had the names been linked into a list structure in alphabetical order, it could require up to seven inspections of cells to identify the one we are looking for.

A binary tree program

The program of Figure 6.21 uses the binary tree structure to store names
in alphabetical order, in the form illustrated in Figure 6.20. The program
reads names, presented in an arbitrary sequence, and adds them succes-
sively to the tree whose root is pointed to by `sort_tree`, using the function `add_to_tree()` to do so. Finally, the function `print_tree()` is used
to print out the names stored in the tree in alphabetical order.

To examine the steps involved in adding a new name to the tree, let
us suppose that the names "Jones", "Brown", and "Smith" have been read
previously, in that order, and we now wish to add the name "Rigby". Figure
6.22 illustrates the state of the tree and its associated pointers at the start
of the execution of the function `add_to_tree()`. The formal parameter
`ptr` (of type 'pointer to pointer to `NODE`') contains the address of the actual
tree root pointer, `sort_tree`, which in turn contains the address of the root
`NODE`, i.e. the node for "Jones", which was the first name read. "Brown",
added subsequently, precedes "Jones" in alphabetical order, and so was
appended to the `left` member of "Jones"; similarly "Smith" was added to
the `right` member.

`add_to_tree()` first searches the tree to find the appropriate branch on
which to append the new name "Rigby". To mark the position identified,
the pointer variable `next` is declared, and is initially set to point to the
root node of the tree. (Note that `ptr` is a pointer to a pointer to a node;
so `*ptr` is a pointer to a node, and it is this pointer (address) that is
assigned to `next`.) Now the new name, "Rigby", is compared with the
name "Jones" that is stored at the node indicated by `next` (`next->name`).
"Rigby" follows "Jones" in alphabetical sequence, so `strcmp()` returns a
positive value, leading to execution of the sequence:

```
ptr = &next->right;
next = next->right;
```

The effect of this is illustrated in the first part of Figure 6.23. The
pointer `next` initially points to the node for "Jones", so `next->right` refers
to the `right` member of this node; `&next->right` is the address of this
member, which is assigned to `ptr`. (Recall that the '`->`' operator has a
higher priority than `&`, so it is applied first.) Note that `ptr`, which is of
type 'pointer to pointer to `NODE`', contains the address of the `right` member
of a node structure, which is of type 'pointer to `NODE`'. The assignment:

```
next = next -> right;
```

however, assigns the pointer-value obtained from the `right` member of
"Jones", to the pointer variable `next`, leaving `next` pointing to the node
that is the right-successor of "Jones".

```
/*
 * This program is an example of the use of a tree
 * (a binary tree in this case) to sort names into
 * alphabetical order. Note that print_tree() is a
 * recursive function.
 */

#include <stdio.h>
#include <stdlib.h>

typedef struct node { char name [26];
                      struct node *left, *right;} NODE;

void add_to_tree(char *new_name, NODE **ptr)
{
   NODE *next = *ptr;

   while (next != NULL)
   {
      if (strcmp(new_name,next->name)<=0)
      {
         ptr = &next->left;
         next = next->left;
      }
      else
      {
         ptr = &next->right;
         next = next->right;
      }
   }

   *ptr = next = malloc( sizeof(NODE) );
   strcpy(next->name,new_name);
   next->left = next->right = NULL;
}

/*------------------------------------------------------*/
```

```
void print_tree(NODE *root)
{
   if (root != NULL)
   {
      print_tree(root->left);
      printf("%s\n",root->name);
      print_tree(root->right);
   }
}

/*-----------------------------------------------------------*/

main()
{
   NODE *sort_tree = NULL;
   char new_name [26];

   printf("Input names to be sorted.\n");
   printf("Each name on a new line.\n* to terminate\n");

   scanf("%25s",new_name);

   while (new_name[0]!='*')
   {
      add_to_tree(new_name,&sort_tree);
      scanf("%25s",new_name);
   }

   print_tree(sort_tree);
}
```

Figure 6.21   An example of the use of a tree, to sort

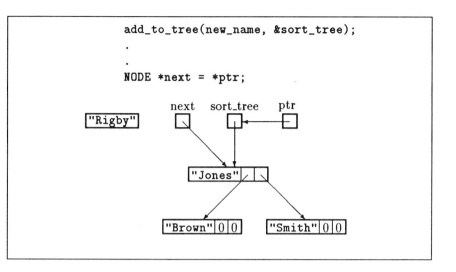

Figure 6.22   Start of function add_to_tree()

The continuation of the comparison sequence is shown in the second part of Figure 6.23. "Rigby" is next compared with the current **next->name**, which is "Smith", and as "Rigby" precedes "Smith" alphabetically, the search continues to the left of "Smith". Again, **ptr** is assigned to contain the *address* of this member, but **next** is assigned the *contents* of the member **next->left**, in this case a null pointer-value. Now we have come to the end of the search; the loop terminates with **next == NULL**, and **ptr** containing the address of the pointer-member to which the new node must be added.

The final stage in **add_to_tree()** is illustrated in Figure 6.24. The library function **malloc()** is called to obtain storage space for the new node, and the pointer **next** is assigned to point to this. The further assignment:

$$*ptr = next;$$

has the effect of assigning this pointer-value also to the pointer variable whose address is contained in **ptr**; i.e. to the **left** member of the node for "Smith", completing the addition to the tree structure. All that remains is to copy the name "Rigby" into the new node (now referenced by **next**) and to initialize its **left** and **right** pointers to **NULL**.

The other function that is included in the program of Figure 6.21, **print_tree()**, illustrates one of the attractive features of dealing with tree structures, especially for this kind of application. In order to print out the names on the tree in alphabetical order, the algorithm required is:

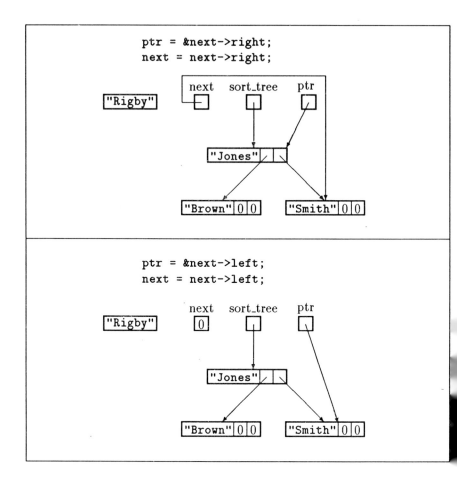

Figure 6.23   Locating a position in the tree

1. Print all the names on the left sub-tree in alphabetical order.

2. Print the name stored at the root node.

3. Print all the names on the right sub-tree in alphabetical order.

The function `print_tree()` implements this algorithm simply and elegantly, using two recursive calls of the same function to print the two sub-trees.

```
*ptr = next = malloc( sizeof(NODE) );
strcpy(next->name,new_name);
next->left = next->right = NULL;
```

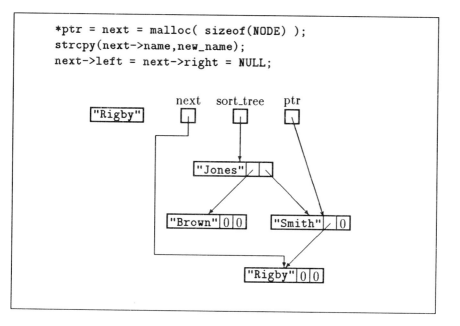

Figure 6.24   Adding the new member

6.4   Unions

We have seen that, in C as in most other high-level languages, the declaration of a variable defines its type, and hence implicitly defines its other attributes. Sometimes, however, it is useful to declare a variable that may assume values of more than one type in different circumstances. In C we can declare a variable to be a **union** of several nominated types.

Suppose, for example, we have previously declared a type COMPLEX thus:

```
typedef struct {float re,im;} COMPLEX;
```

Then the union declaration:

```
union data {int integer;float real;COMPLEX complex;} d1,d2;
```

declares two variables, d1 and d2, whose type is **union data**. The values that may be assumed by these variables may be any of the three types **int**, **float** and COMPLEX defined as **members** of the union.

Notice the similarity of this declaration to that of a structure. In fact, the syntax associated with the use of unions is essentially the same as that for structures; the semantic difference, however, is that whereas the members of a structure define different variables, the members of a union define different possible manifestations of the same variable. It is the responsibility of the programmer to remember which type is currently assumed by a union variable, and to use it appropriately. The sizes of the types that are members of a union need not all be the same; sufficient storage space is allocated to accommodate the largest type listed.

The general form of a union declaration follows that for structures:

union < *union tag* > { < *member list* > } < *variable list* >;

As with structures, the < *union tag* > may be omitted when declaring variables of an unnamed union type, or the < *variable list* > may be omitted when declaring a type that is to be used later.

When a reference is made to a variable that is of a union type, the name of a member of a union is appended to indicate which type-manifestation is being used:

< *union variable name* >.< *member name* >

For example, we would write:

```
d1.integer
```

to refer to the variable **d1** in its **int** type manifestation. Again, the notation used is like that used for structures, and we also use:

< *pointer to union* >-><< *member name* >

to refer to a member of a union accessed via a pointer variable.

Figure 6.25 illustrates the use of union variables. This program uses a structure, given the name **EXPRESSION**, which might be used in a program such as a compiler to store the details of an arithmetic expression. The members of the structure are a **char**, named **operator**, which defines the operator-symbol used in the expression, and two subsidiary member-structures, to define the two operands (**pre** and **post**). Operands may be of three kinds: single-character variables, integer numeric values, or bracketed sub-expressions of the same form. To represent an operand, the structure **op_descript** contains two members: **type**, used to define which of the three kinds is this operand, and a union, **operand**, used to store the actual operand representation. The members of the union, therefore, correspond to the three different kinds of operand: **char var**, to represent an operand that is a variable identifier; **int num**, representing a numeric value; and **struct expr *expr**, to store a pointer to a sub-expression of the **struct expr** form.

```
/* This program is an example of the use of a union.
 * A structure 'EXPRESSION' is defined which can store an
 * arithmetic expression.
 * Each operand of the expression is stored in a union. The
 * union allows for variables, integer constants and sub
 * expressions. */

#include <stdio.h>

#define VAR 0
#define NUM 1
#define EXPR 2

typedef struct expr
        { char operator;
          struct op_descript
             { int type;
               union op {char var; int num;
                           struct expr *expr; } operand;
             } pre, post;
        } EXPRESSION;

typedef struct op_descript OP_DESCRIPT;

void print_expression(EXPRESSION *);
void print_sub_expr(EXPRESSION *);
void print_operand(OP_DESCRIPT *);

/*-----------------------------------------------------------*/

main()
{ /* setting up some expressions 'by hand' for
   * demonstration purposes */

  EXPRESSION e1,e2,e3;

  e1.operator = '+';
  e1.pre.type = VAR;
  e1.pre.operand.var = 'x';
  e1.post.type = NUM;
  e1.post.operand.num = 5;
```

```
        e2.operator = '-';
        e2.pre.type = VAR;
        e2.pre.operand.var = 'y';
        e2.post.type = VAR;
        e2.post.operand.var = 'z';

        e3.operator = '*';
        e3.pre.type = EXPR;
        e3.pre.operand.expr = &e1;
        e3.post.type = EXPR;
        e3.post.operand.expr = &e2;

        print_expression(&e3); printf("\n");
}

/*-------------------------------------------------------------*/

void print_expression(EXPRESSION *e)
{
    if (e->pre.type == EXPR)
        print_sub_expr(e->pre.operand.expr);
    else print_operand(&e->pre);

    printf("%c",e->operator);

    if (e->post.type == EXPR)
        print_sub_expr(e->post.operand.expr);
    else print_operand(&e->post);
}

/*-------------------------------------------------------------*/

void print_sub_expr(EXPRESSION *e)
{
    printf("(");
    print_expression(e);
    printf(")");
}

/*-------------------------------------------------------------*/
```

```
void print_operand(OP_DESCRIPT *oper)
{
    switch(oper->type)
    {
        case VAR: printf("%c",oper->operand.var);
                  break;
        case NUM: printf("%-d",oper->operand.num);
                  break;
        default:  printf("*** something's gone wrong!!! ***");
    }
}
```

Figure 6.25   Example of the use of union

The program of Figure 6.25 is written for illustrative purposes only, so the main() function simply initializes some variables of the EXPRESSION structure and then prints out their values. The initialization of the variable e1 is represented pictorially in Figure 6.26.

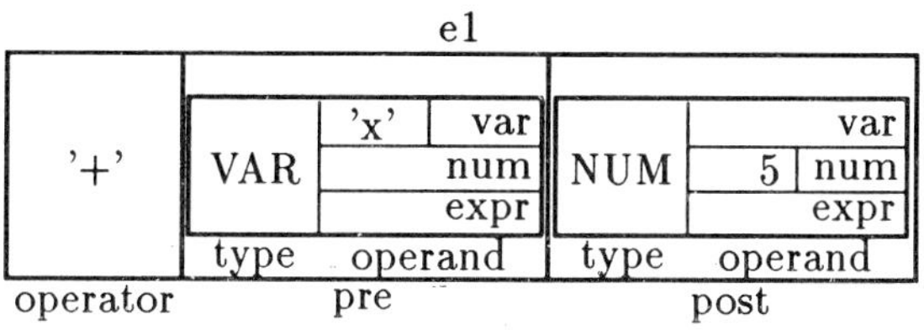

Figure 6.26   The structure EXPRESSION — containing a union

The data structure for e1 comprises three members: the operator, in this case the character '+', and the representations of the operands, pre and post. Each of these in turn comprises two parts: the type of the operand, and its representation, operand. In the case of pre, the type member is given the value VAR (defined to be equivalent to the integer 0), by the assignment:

$$e1.pre.type = VAR;$$

Notice the double application of the '.' operator: e1.pre refers to the member **pre** of **e1**; this is itself a structure, of which **e1.pre.type** is one member. Similarly, the assignment:

e1.post.type = NUM;

defines the second operand to be of the numeric kind.

The second member of the structure **op_descript** is the union, **operand**, which has three alternative manifestations: **var**, **num** or **expr**. In the case of **e1.pre**, the **type** member has been given the value **VAR**, so it is appropriate to give the **operand** member a value of the corresponding member-type, **var**. This is done by the assignment:

e1.pre.operand.var = 'x';

Here, **e1.pre.operand** refers to the **operand** member of the structure which is the **pre** member of **e1**; **e1.pre.operand.var** refers to the member **var** of the union **operand**, i.e. to **operand** in its manifestation as a value of type **char**.

The whole structure thus initialized, and visualized in Figure 6.26, represents the expression **x+5**. Using the operand **type expr**, however, it is possible to include as terms in an expression pointers to other expressions. The structure for **e2** defined in Figure 6.25 represents the expression **y−z**, and the structure for **e3** represents **e1*e2**, using the assignments:

e3.pre.operand.expr = &e1;
e3.post.operand.expr = &e2;

to set up pointers to the two other expression structures. The complex of structures representing **(x+5)*(y−z)** may be visualized as a tree, illustrated in Figure 6.27.

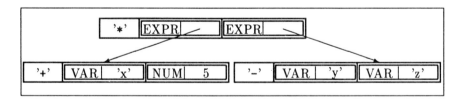

Figure 6.27   Using structures and unions to represent(x+5)*(y−z)

Note, finally, that it is always necessary for the programmer to make separate provision for the different cases corresponding to alternative members of a union. We see this, for example, in the function **print_operand()** of Figure 6.25, which distinguishes the two alternative cases being dealt with by examining the **type** member of the structure, in order to choose the appropriate form of **printf()** call required to print the corresponding **operand**.

Bit fields

In certain kinds of application, it is necessary to define structures comprising a number of members, each of which can have only a limited range of values. Often, for example, a structure includes numbers that are essentially binary 'flags', recording which of two cases applies to the data represented by the structure. In such applications, it may be important to minimize the storage requirements by representing several of these members within a single word of store. The C language facility of **bit fields** allows us to do this.

A member of a structure is specified to be stored as a bit field by appending an integer constant:

$$: < number\ of\ bits >$$

to the declaration of the appropriate identifier. For example:

```
struct record{unsigned sex:1;unsigned age:7;
        unsigned number_of_children:3;}someone;
```

declares **someone** to be a variable whose type is **struct record**, comprising three bit-field members: **sex**, which is stored as a single bit, **age**, which is stored in seven bits, and **number_of_children**, for which three bits are required. The type used for the bit-field members must be integer, and is usually, as in this case, **unsigned**. Bit fields are referenced in exactly the same way as the other members of a structure: the only difference is that the compiler will, in implementation-dependent ways, attempt to store their values by packing them into words in an efficient way.

Figure 6.28 illustrates a typical use of bit fields. Notice that the structure **PERSON** contains a mixture of bit fields and others.

The main advantage of using bit fields, rather than the alternative of encoding values in a word which is then unpacked using bitwise operators, is that assignments such as:

```
individual->sex = sex;
```

can be performed directly, without having to specify the bit manipulations involved. Beware, however, of trying to mix bit-field operations and bitwise operations; the way in which bit fields are allocated within words of store is implementation-dependent.

```
/* This program illustrates the use of bit fields.
 * Census data is being kept which requires the following
 * information to be stored for each person in the census:
 *
 * Name
 * Sex                (Male/Female)
 * Marital status     (Single/Married/Widowed/Divorced)
 * Employment status  (Under age/Working/Unemployed/Retired)
 */

#include <stdio.h>
#include <stdlib.h>

typedef struct {char *name; unsigned sex:1;
      unsigned mar_status:2; unsigned work_status:2;}PERSON;

/* sexes */
#define MALE     0
#define FEMALE   1

/* marital status */
#define SINGLE   0
#define MARRIED  1
#define DIVORCED 2
#define WIDOWED  3

/* work status */
#define UNDER_AGE  0
#define WORKING    1
#define UNEMPLOYED 2
#define RETIRED    3

int set_up_test_data(PERSON **);
void set_up(PERSON *, char *, unsigned, unsigned, unsigned);
void print_sing_unem(PERSON *, int);

/*------------------------------------------------------------*/
```

```
main()
{
    PERSON *people;
    int number;

    number = set_up_test_data(&people);

    print_sing_unem(people,number);
}

/*----------------------------------------------------------*/

int set_up_test_data(PERSON **census_data)
{
    PERSON *p;
#define NUM 7

    *census_data = p = malloc(NUM*sizeof(PERSON));

    set_up(&p[0],"K Chan",MALE,MARRIED,WORKING);
    set_up(&p[1],"C Charlton",MALE,SINGLE,UNEMPLOYED);
    set_up(&p[2],"P E Dunne",MALE,MARRIED,WORKING);
    set_up(&p[3],"D Jackson",MALE,MARRIED,RETIRED);
    set_up(&p[4],"P Leng",MALE,SINGLE,UNEMPLOYED);
    set_up(&p[5],"J Little",FEMALE,SINGLE,UNEMPLOYED);
    set_up(&p[6],"J Watt",MALE,MARRIED,WORKING);

    return NUM;
}

/*----------------------------------------------------------*/

void set_up(PERSON *individual, char *nom, unsigned sex,
                        unsigned mstatus, unsigned wstatus)
{
    individual->name = malloc(strlen(nom)+1);
    strcpy(individual->name,nom);
    individual->sex = sex;
    individual->mar_status = mstatus;
    individual->work_status = wstatus;
}

/*----------------------------------------------------------*/
```

```
void print_sing_unem(PERSON *population, int num)
{
    int i;

    printf("A List of the SINGLE who are UNEMPLOYED:\n");

    for (i=0; i<num; i++)
    {
        if (population[i].mar_status==SINGLE &&
            population[i].work_status==UNEMPLOYED)
        printf("%s\n",population[i].name);
    }
}
```

Figure 6.28   Structures with bit fields

6.5   Exercises

1. Extend the program of Figure 6.2 to include a function that generates a
   list of items to be ordered according to the current stock levels recorded.
       An item should be ordered if the actual stock level for that item is
   less than the set 'min_level' for the item.
       For such items, the number ordered should restore the stock level,
   for that item, to twice the 'min_level'.

2. Write a function to calculate the total duration of two time periods.
   Each is represented by a set of three integers corresponding to hours,
   minutes and seconds respectively.

3. Extend the set of 'complex' functions of Figure 6.7 to include a complex
   multiply function.

4. Write a function that determines the value of a number input as a sequence of Roman numerals whose values are:

$$
\begin{array}{rl}
\text{I} & :1 \\
\text{V} & :5 \\
\text{X} & :10 \\
\text{L} & :50
\end{array}
$$

C : 100
D : 500
M : 1000

The value of a Roman number is obtained by adding the values of its numerals, except where a numeral (R) has to its right a numeral of greater value than R, in which case the value of R is subtracted. For example, **MCMXIX** represents 1919.

5. Set up an enumerated data type to represent the months of the year. Use your data type in a function that, when given today's date, will deliver tomorrow's date. A date consists of the day followed by the month, e.g. **31 January**.

6. Extend the 'visitor book' program (Figures 6.11, 6.12, 6.15, 6.18) so that the number of visits that a person has made is recorded. (You need only record times of the current (or last) visit.)

7. A printer queue contains the following information for each job:

   - job number;
   - job size (in blocks);
   - time it was requested.

   New jobs are added to the end of the queue, while jobs are removed from the front of the queue when they have been completed, always in the order in which they arrived.
   Write a function to add a job to the end of the queue. Assume that job descriptions (in the form of job number and size) are given as input to the program, which should then determine the time of each request for addition to the queue.
   Write a second function to remove a completed job from the front of the queue. In order to determine when a job is ready for removal your program should wait for some random time interval, representing the execution time of the job at the head of the queue.

8. Extend the tree sort program of Figure 6.21 to include a function which counts the number of names (NODEs) on a tree or sub-tree.
   Rewrite the function **add_to_tree()** to make it recursive.

9. Write a program to store the names of British rivers and their tributaries using a binary tree. Rivers should be ordered alphabetically on the tree, as should the tributaries of each river.
   (**Hint:** in order to allow a waterway to have any number of tributaries,

each node must point to the first of its tributaries and to a sibling waterway.)

Write a function to print out the tributaries of a given waterway and another to print out the waterway to which a given tributary belongs.

10. Design a structure to record information about a set of 'things'. For each thing you should record (a) its name, and (b) if it is animal, vegetable or mineral.

If it is an animal, record (a) the number of legs it has, (b) whether it can fly or not, and (c) whether it primarily lives in water or on land.

If it is a vegetable, record (a) its colour, (b) whether it naturally occurs in the United Kingdom, (c) if it is edible, and (d) which of the following groups it belongs to (tree/vegetable/weed/other).

If it is a mineral, record (a) its cost per pound, and (b) whether it is man-made or naturally occurring.

Test your structure by writing a test input and output function for it.

Chapter 7

Pointers to functions

7.1 Function pointers

As we have seen, the ANSI C language has two central concepts: the concept of a **function**, which performs some defined algorithmic actions on program variables, and the concept of a **variable**, which has an **address**, a **type**, and a **value** that may be accessed and manipulated by the actions of functions.

In some current high-level languages, the two concepts are essentially unified, providing the notion of a function, or procedure, as a 'first-class object' that can be manipulated just like any other program value. While this is not so in the C language, C *does* allow us to define pointers to functions, and in this way to achieve many of the effects of 'functions as variables'.

Suppose, for example, we are writing a program that is to execute arithmetic expressions interpretatively, reading the expressions in textual form and performing appropriate operations. We might find it useful to define a structure in which one member represents the operation code symbol (e.g. '+', or '*') and the other member *points* to the function written to carry out the corresponding operation. A table of these structures could then be used to look up and invoke the action required to execute a given operation.

We could declare a pointer to a function of this kind thus:

```
float(*command)(float,float);
```

This declares command to be a pointer to a function that takes two parameters, each of type **float**, and returns a result of type **float**. In general, the declaration has the form:

$< result\ type > (* < function\ pointer\ name >) (< parameter\ types >)$

The parentheses enclosing the pointer name are necessary to distinguish this from a normal function definition, and those enclosing the parameter list to establish this as a *function* pointer in particular. The enclosed list of parameter types may, however, be omitted, in which case no check for parameter-type compatibility is made.

Once declared, a function pointer can be assigned to point to a defined function:

```
command = multiply;
        /* 'multiply' has been declared as a function */
```

and then the function can be called via its pointer:

```
result = (*command)(x,y);
```

This call will have the effect of invoking the function multiply(), with actual parameters x and y, to deliver a result which is assigned to result.

```
/* This program illustrates how pointers to functions can
 * be declared, assigned to and used to call a function.  */
#include <stdio.h>

/*------------------------------------------------------------*/

void test(int data)
{ printf("number= %d\n",data); }

/*------------------------------------------------------------*/

main()
{
    void (*fun_ptr)(int);   /* declare function pointer */
    fun_ptr= test;          /* assign function to pointer */
    (*fun_ptr)(1);          /* call function via pointer */
}
```

Figure 7.1   A simple example of a function pointer

Figure 7.1 shows a simple case of the definition of a function pointer, its assignment to point to a function, and the call of the function using the pointer.

The application of function pointers in the implementation of an expression interpreter is developed more fully in Figure 7.2. Here, the function pointer declaration has been incorporated into a structure declaration:

```
typedef struct{char id;
        float (*command)(float,float);}COMMAND_ENTRY;
```

This enables the declaration of a table of these structures, in which the single-character operator-identifiers are associated with pointers to the functions plus(), minus(), etc. A pointer com_ptr is used to point to an entry in this table, and a function is called by the statement:

```
result = (*com_ptr->command)(op1,op2);
```

```c
/* This program illustrates how a pointer to a function can
 * be part of a structure. */

#include <stdio.h>
#define BOOL int
#define FALSE 0
#define TRUE 1

/*------------------------------------------------------------*/

float plus (float num1, float num2)
{
    return num1+num2;
}

/*------------------------------------------------------------*/

float minus (float num1, float num2)
{
    return num1-num2;
}

/*------------------------------------------------------------*/
```

```
float times (float num1, float num2)
{
   return num1*num2;
}

/*-----------------------------------------------------------*/

float divide (float num1, float num2)
{
   return num1/num2;
}

/*-----------------------------------------------------------*/

float dummy(float num1, float num2)
{
   printf("** This should never get called\n");
}

/*-----------------------------------------------------------*/

typedef struct{char id;
               float (*command)(float, float);}COMMAND_ENTRY;

COMMAND_ENTRY command_table [] =
{
   { '+',plus},
   { '-',minus},
   { '*',times},
   { '/',divide},
   { '.',dummy}
};

/*-----------------------------------------------------------*/
```

```
#define TERMINATOR '.'

main()
{
    BOOL notfound, notend=TRUE;
    COMMAND_ENTRY *com_ptr;
    char operator;
    float op1,op2;

    printf("input simple expressions in the form:\n");
    printf("<operator> <operand> <operand>\n");
    printf("%c to terminate\n",TERMINATOR);

    while (notend)
    {
        notfound = TRUE;
        com_ptr = command_table;
        scanf(" %c",&operator);
        if (operator!=TERMINATOR) scanf(" %f %f",&op1,&op2);
        while (notfound && com_ptr->id != TERMINATOR)
        {
            if (com_ptr->id==operator)
            {
                float result;
                notfound=FALSE;
                result = (*com_ptr->command)(op1,op2);
                printf("= %f\n",result);
            }
            else com_ptr++;
        }
        if (operator=='.') notend = FALSE;
        else if (notfound) printf("** illegal command **\n");
    }
}
```

Figure 7.2   The use of a function pointer as a member of a structure

Functions as function-arguments

Another application of function pointers occurs when we wish to invoke a function with another function as a parameter.

Figure 7.3 illustrates this possibility. Here we have declared a function `sum_series()`, that adds together a sequence of terms calculated by the successive application of a function, a pointer to which is passed as a parameter to `sum_series()`. In the `main()` function, `sum_series()` is called, first to sum a series using the function `quadratic()`, and then to sum a series using the library function `sin()`. Notice that the *name* of the function (e.g. `sin`), used as an actual parameter, defines a pointer to the function; the formal parameter name is `func`, given the parameter specification:

```
double (*func)(double)
```

and the function is invoked using this name:

```
total += (*func)(pt);
```

Figure 7.3 illustrates the way we can use function pointers to implement **generic** functions, to perform some generalized algorithm (such as, in this case, summing a series), the details of which are augmented by the particular parameterization. We can also use function parameters as a way of implementing **polymorphic** functions; i.e., functions that perform an algorithm on data of different types. An example of this is the function `qsort()`, which is provided as part of the ANSI standard library. The `qsort()` function is an implementation of the 'quicksort' algorithm, to sort a table of data into order. The nature of the information in the table, and the basis on which it is to be ordered, are specified explicitly and implicitly in the parameters to `qsort()`:

```
void qsort (void *base;size_t nel;size_t size;
            int (*compare)(const void *,const void *))
```

Here, the parameters `base`, `nel` and `size` define respectively the base address of the table, the number of elements in the table, and the size in bytes of a single element. The parameter `compare` is a pointer to a function which is required to compare two elements, returning the result:

<0	when its first argument precedes its second argument
=0	when its arguments are equal
>0	when its first argument follows its second argument

Notice, however, that the types of the arguments of `compare()` are not defined in the parameter specification of `qsort()`; this is so that the

```
/* This program illustrates passing a function as an
 * argument to a function. It achieves this by using
 * pointers to functions. /*
#include <stdio.h>
#include <math.h>

/*---------------------------------------------------*/

double sum_series(double from, double to, double by,
                                  double (*func)(double) )
{
    double total=0, pt;

    for (pt=from; pt<=to; pt+=by) total += (*func)(pt);

    return total;
}

/*---------------------------------------------------*/

main()
{
    double result;
    double quadratic(double), sin(double);

    printf("Summing series\n\n");
    result=sum_series(1, 100, 0.5, quadratic);
    printf("2x**2 + 4x - 3 summed from x=1 to x=100 ");
    printf("in steps of 0.5 = %f\n",result);
    result=sum_series(0, 1.5, 0.01, sin);
    printf("sin(x) summed from x=0 to x=1.5 ");
    printf("in steps of 0.01 = %f\n",result);
}

/*---------------------------------------------------*/

double quadratic(double x)
{ return 2*x*x + 4*x - 3; }
```

Figure 7.3 A function as an argument to a function—sum_series()

function supplied as an *actual* parameter can be either (say) a numeric-comparison function, or a function to compare two strings alphabetically. (The library function strcmp() has the necessary specification.) The function qsort() is therefore polymorphic in that it can sort into order values of any type, subject to the ordering determined by its function-pointer parameter.

Figure 7.4 illustrates the use of the qsort() function. A table has been set up to contain the names and examination marks of a class of students. The main() function first of all prints out the table in alphabetical order of student names, then in examination mark order. It does so by first calling the function qsort() to sort the table into alphabetical order:

```
qsort(class_of_59,NUM_STUDENTS,
                    sizeof(STUDENT),name_compare);
```

For this call, the function-pointer parameter to qsort() is the function name_compare(), which calls the library function strcmp() to compare two strings corresponding to student names. When the table is subsequently to be sorted into numerical mark order, qsort() is called with a pointer to the function mark_compare() as its last parameter. This function refers to the same data structure STUDENT, but compares table entries on the basis of the numerical order of the mark members.

7.2   Exercises

1. Construct a table that houses information about the performance of share prices on the stock market for a group of computer companies. For each company the information stored comprises: the company name, current share price (in dollars) and the highest and lowest share values in the last 12 months. Sample data is:

Name	share price	12month high	12month low
DEC	55.5	81.75	49.5
HP	58.5	60	30.75
IBM	90.88	139.5	84.88
Sun	30.88	38.25	21.25

Your program should allow the table to be sorted on the proportion of the differential high–low price that the current price reflects.

```
/* This program illustrates the use of the library function
 * 'qsort'. 'qsort' requires to be told how to compare
 * entries. This is done by supplying an argument which is
 * a pointer to a function. */

#include <stdio.h>
#include <stdlib.h>

typedef struct{char name[21];int mark;}STUDENT;

STUDENT class_of_59 []=
{
    {"Smith J",45},
    {"Bailey J M",76},
    {"Jermyn J",83},
    {"Powell B",47},
    {"Wilcox M",50},
    {"Fisher A C",65},
    {"Wilcox K",55},
    {"Charlton C C",23},
    {"Baker A",52},
    {"Plant R",58},
    {"Leyland K",57},
    {"Griffiths D",44},
    {"Massey K",76}
};
#define NUM_STUDENTS 13

/*----------------------------------------------------------*/

int name_compare(STUDENT *a, STUDENT *b)
{ return strcmp(a->name, b->name); }

/*----------------------------------------------------------*/
```

```
int mark_compare(STUDENT *a, STUDENT *b)
{
   int mark1 = a->mark, mark2 = b->mark;

   if (mark1>mark2) return -1;
   if (mark1==mark2) return 0;
   else return 1;
}

/*----------------------------------------------------------*/

main()
{
   int i;
   STUDENT *ptr;

   printf("Students and marks in alphabetical order\n\n");

   qsort(class_of_59, NUM_STUDENTS,
                      sizeof(STUDENT), name_compare);

   ptr = class_of_59;
   for (i=0; i<NUM_STUDENTS; ptr++,i++)
      printf("%-20s%2d\n",ptr->name,ptr->mark);

   printf("\n\nStudents and marks in mark rank order\n\n");

   qsort(class_of_59, NUM_STUDENTS,
                      sizeof(STUDENT), mark_compare);

   ptr = class_of_59;
   for (i=0; i<NUM_STUDENTS; ptr++,i++)
      printf("%-20s%2d\n",ptr->name,ptr->mark);
}
```

Figure 7.4   An example of the use of qsort()

2. Extend the program of Figure 7.4 so that the data structure STUDENT also houses the sex of the student.

Now write compare routines which would enable the class to be sorted:

(a) alphabetically, but girls prior to boys;

(b) in mark rank order, but girls prior to boys.

3. Write a program to implement a simple word-processing system. The program should take as input a text file in which any of a set of commands may be embedded. Each command must be preceded by the > symbol and must occur at the start of a line. Valid commands are:

>P : begin new paragraph
>S : begin a new section, using the remaining text on the current line as the section header
>N : begin a new page
>L : convert the remaining text on the current line to lower case
>U : convert the remaining text on the current line to upper case

Paragraphs should be separated by a blank line and should begin with an indented line. Section headings should be centralized and underlined, and followed by three blank lines.

4. Write a generalized merge function capable of merging two tables of data, each of which is already sorted. Your function should work for tables of any data type.

Use your function in a program to merge two football league tables based on the number of points gained by each team.

5. Write a generalized function which tests to see if a particular 'node' is already on an ordered binary tree. Nodes of the tree should have three parts:

(a) A structure which contains the 'user' information stored at the node.

(b) A pointer to a sub-tree containing all the nodes that come before this node.

(c) A pointer to a sub-tree containing all the nodes that come after this node.

If a match of the node being searched for is found, your function should deliver a pointer (void *) to the node on the tree that matches. Otherwise, a NULL pointer should be returned.

Your function will need the following arguments:

(a) A pointer to the tree to be searched.

(b) A pointer to the structure containing the information to be compared.

(c) The byte size of the structure holding the 'user' information at a node.

(d) A pointer to a function which can indicate the ordering of two sets of node information (before, same, or after).

Adapt the program of Figure 6.21 to make it suitable to test your 'on_tree()' function.

Chapter 8

Mixed-language programming

8.1   C and other languages

Most programs are wholly written in a single language. Each programming language, however, has its own strengths and weaknesses, and the choice of language to implement a particular task is often a compromise that may be less than ideal. A language such as Pascal offers greater expressive power than assembly language, but it may be necessary to use the latter to interface the program to a specialized hardware device, or to obtain the speed of execution required. Another language, such as FORTRAN, may be desirable simply because of the availability of libraries of pre-written routines in that language.

For these reasons, sometimes the best solution is to use a mixture of languages in a single program. Because C has some of the characteristics of both high-level and low-level languages, it is often the best choice for the 'base' language in this kind of application, to be used to write the main program within which portions written in other languages may be included. In practice, these program parts will almost invariably be defined as routines, or functions.

To enable a program written in one language to incorporate routines in a different language, it is necessary that the two compilers should adhere to common conventions in a number of respects, and that the linker should accept separately compiled routines from both sources. Often this is the case when a particular software supplier provides a range of compilers to a common standard, or when different suppliers all accept the conventions defined by a particular linker and operating system. Even when mixed-language programming is feasible, however, it is still necessary to ensure that the parameter-passing conventions of the routine and its calling program are reconciled, and it is to this issue that we give particular attention in this chapter.

8.2   FORTRAN77

It is often reasonably straightforward to call a FORTRAN77 subroutine or function from within a C program, provided that the compilers produce object code in a common format, and adhere to common conventions for the processing of arguments and returning of results. As in all mixed-language programming, it is necessary to consult local documentation to ensure that correct procedures are followed for compiling and linking the program routines, and to avoid problems which may arise from implementation-specific details. Aside from these, the major difficulty concerns the different parameter-passing mechanisms of the two languages. As we know, ANSI C uses **call-by-value** in all cases, whereas FORTRAN employs a **call-by-reference** mechanism in which the function argument is the address of the actual parameter.

Consider the C program of Figure 8.1. The program includes a function, min_max(), which takes three parameters: **array**, a pointer to an array of integers; **largest**, a pointer to a variable used to contain the value found to be the largest in the array; and **n**, the size of the array. All three are 'value' parameters, but in two cases the values passed are in fact pointers, allowing the effect of call-by-reference to be obtained. The parameter **n**, however, is an actual value, which does not correspond to any program variable in the calling environment; the function-calling mechanism of C defines a variable **n**, local to the function min_max(), which is assigned an initial value corresponding to the value passed as the actual parameter.

Figure 8.2 illustrates a possible FORTRAN implementation of the function min_max() that, let us suppose, we wish to call from within a C program. The parameters **ARRAY** and **LARGEST** will pose no problems, since the FORTRAN call-by-reference mechanism is compatible with the use of pointer-value parameters in C. To deal with the parameter **N**, however, it is necessary for the C program, in this case, to define a variable the address of which can be the actual parameter—converting the original call-by-value into an effective call-by-reference. Figure 8.3 illustrates the form of program required to replace the **main()** function of Figure 8.1.

```c
/* A function to deliver the largest and smallest number
 * in an array might be written in C as follows: */
#include <stdio.h>
#define LENGTH 7
int data[] = { 17, 21, 5, 43, 121, 12, 3 };

int min_max(int *array,int n, int *largest)
{
  int big,little;

  big = little = *array++;
  n--;
  while (n>0)
  {
     int temp = *array++;

     if (temp>big) big=temp;
     else if (temp<little) little =temp;

     n--;
  }
  *largest = big;
  return little;
}

/*----------------------------------------------------------*/

/* To call a C version of min_max */

main()
{
   int min, max;

   if (LENGTH>0) min = min_max(data, LENGTH, &max);
   else exit(1);

   printf("minimum = %d maximum = %d\n",min,max);
}
```

Figure 8.1   A program including a function, min_max()

```
C       This function is going to be called by a C program.
C
        INTEGER FUNCTION MIN_MAX( ARRAY, N, LARGEST)
C       .. Scalar Arguments ..
        INTEGER            N, LARGEST
C       .. Array Arguments ..
        INTEGER ARRAY( * )
C       .. Local Scalars ..
        INTEGER BIG, LITTLE, TEMP
C       .. Executable Statements ..
        BIG = ARRAY(1)
        LITTLE = BIG
        DO 10, I=2, N, 1
           TEMP = ARRAY(I)
           IF (TEMP .GT. BIG) THEN
              BIG = TEMP
           ELSE IF (TEMP .LT. LITTLE) THEN
              LITTLE = TEMP
           END IF
    10 CONTINUE
C
        LARGEST = BIG
        MIN_MAX = LITTLE
        RETURN
C
C       End of MIN_MAX
C
        END
```

Figure 8.2   A FORTRAN implementation of min_max()

```
/* This program illustrates making a call compatible
 * with FORTRAN's call by reference.*/
#include <stdio.h>

extern int min_max(int *, int *, int *);

int data[] = { 17, 21, 5, 43, 121, 12, 3 };
#define LENGTH 7

/* To call a FORTRAN version of min_max */
main()
{
    int min, max, length;

    if (LENGTH>0)
    {
        int length = LENGTH;
        min = min_max(data, &length, &max);
    }
    else exit(1);

    printf("minimum = %d maximum = %d\n",min,max);
}
```

Figure 8.3   A C program to call the FORTRAN function

8.3   Pascal

Pascal employs both call-by-reference (**var** parameters) and call-by-value. As we have seen, both of these mechanisms can be emulated in C, so simple parameter-passing between a C program and a Pascal function presents few problems. Greater difficulties are encountered in dealing with arrays and other multiple values as parameters and results of functions. Pascal passes array-type parameters in the form of descriptors, the structure of which is implementation-dependent. Provided this structure is known, however, it may be possible to mimic the parameter form required using C value parameters.

Figure 8.4 shows a possible implementation in Pascal of the function min_max() that we have been using for illustration in this chapter. The

```
{ This function is going to be called by a C program. }
module pas;

export
function min_max(numbers:array [lwb..upb:integer] of integer;
                                 var big: integer):integer;
implement
function min_max(numbers:array [lwb..upb:integer] of integer;
                                 var big: integer):integer;

var small, i, temp :integer;
begin
   small := numbers[lwb];
   big := small;
   for i:= lwb+1 to upb do
   begin
      temp := numbers[i];
      if temp>big then
         big := temp
      else if temp<small then
         small := temp
   end;
   min_max := small
end;
end.
```

Figure 8.4   A Pascal implementation of min_max()

Pascal function is packaged in the form of a **module** for external use;
we will assume that the external name to be used to refer to the function is obtained by concatenating the module name and the function name
to produce **pas_min_max()**,although this is an implementation-dependent
characteristic.

The Pascal function has two parameters: **numbers**, which is an array
of integers with associated lower and upper bounds, and **big**, which is a
variable-type (call-by-reference) integer parameter. If we wish to call the
function from within a C program, we need to know the structure of the
array descriptor which is used to define the parameter **numbers**. Let us
suppose that this structure takes the form of a sequence of four simple

values, defining, in order, the lower bound of the array, the upper bound of
the array, the size in bytes of each element, and the address of the array.
We are then able to mimic this descriptor using a C function call with four
equivalent simple actual parameters to correspond to the four elements
required.

```
/* This program illustrates a calling sequence compatible
 * for use with a Pascal function. */

#include <stdio.h>

extern int pas_min_max(int, int, int, int *, int *);

int data[] = { 17, 21, 5, 43, 121, 12, 3 };
#define LENGTH 7


/* To call a Pascal version of min_max */

main()
{
    int min, max, echo=0;

    asm_initproc(&echo); /* Pascal initialization routine */

    if (LENGTH>0) min = pas_min_max(1,LENGTH,4,data,&max);
    else exit(1);

    printf("minimum = %d maximum = %d\n",min,max);

    asm_wrapup(); /* Pascal close routine */
}
```

Figure 8.5   A C program to call the Pascal function

Figure 8.5 shows a possible C program to call this function. The first
four actual parameters of the call of **pas_min_max()** represent the elements
of the descriptor corresponding to the formal parameter **numbers**; the final
pointer parameter, **max**, corresponds to the variable parameter **big** of the
Pascal function.

It is hardly necessary to repeat how implementation-dependent these
details are. We include them here to demonstrate the possibility, available
because of the simplicity of C's parameter-passing mechanism, of working
around the more complex mechanisms required by other languages, to produce equivalent effects. For this to be possible, it is of course necessary first
to obtain the relevant details of the local implementation of the language
concerned.

Another feature of the program of Figure 8.5 illustrates another aspect of system dependency. The program makes a call to a library function, `asm_initproc()`, at its start, and concludes with a call to a function
`asm_wrapup()`. These functions are required (in the implementation we
are using) to initialize and terminate the Pascal run-time system which is
used by any Pascal functions invoked. Again, these are system-dependent
features, the details of which can only be found by reference to the local
documentation of the system being used.

8.4   Assembly language

Incorporating routines written in assembly language into a C program in-
volves, of course, a degree of system dependency even greater than that
associated with other forms of mixed-language programming, and for this
reason it is difficult to offer any rules that apply in general. Unfortunately,
there are sometimes occasions when the use of assembly language is un-
avoidable, in order to obtain low-level control of a particular device, or to
speed up the execution of a critical program section. For those readers who
may encounter this requirement, we will discuss some of the issues raised in
a particular machine and language implementation, in the hope that these
may offer some guidelines for use in other contexts.

The first requirement, if we are to write a routine in assembly language,
is an understanding of the architecture of the target machine we are using. In our case, this is a system based on the Motorola 68000 processor,
which is used in a very wide variety of computers. In order to write an
assembly language program for this machine, we require a detailed understanding of the 68000 processor characteristics, but we need say here only
that the 68000 includes eight 32-bit data registers, d0–d7, and eight 32-bit
address registers, a0–a7. One of the latter, a7, is used to define the top of
a workspace stack that 'grows' from high to low addresses.

If we are to use an assembly language routine within a C program,
we need to know not only the details of the machine architecture and the
assembly language but also the details of the ways in which the C language
implementation makes use of the target machine. Of particular importance

is the way in which registers are used and memory space is organized, because failure to observe equivalent conventions in our assembly language routine could have catastrophic results.

In the implementation of C we are considering, the principal relevant details of register use are the following:

1. Register a6 is used to define a current stack frame: local variables and parameters are addressed relative to this base.

2. Registers d0, d1, a0 and a1 are treated as working registers, available for use within routines without restriction. The other registers, d2–d7 and a2–a5, may be used for **register** variables within the C program, so any use within an external routine must preserve and restore their values.

3. The result of a function is returned in register d0 (for values up to 32 bits) or d0 and d1 (for larger values).

Store is allocated for local variables and routine parameters using the stack, so it is within this structure that our assembly language routines must work for all except global-variable access. The sequence used when a function is called is as follows:

1. Actual parameters are pushed onto the stack in reverse order.

2. The function is invoked by a subroutine call (the 68000 **jsr** instruction).

3. Within the function routine, the 68000 **link** instruction is used to allocate local data space and to set up the frame base register, a6, and the stack top register, a7. The previous value of a6 is saved on the stack, and the new value can be used to reference the stacked parameters and the newly-allocated local workspace.

Figure 8.6 illustrates the state of the stack following a function call. The frame base pointer (a6) points to the (four-byte) location containing the previous value of this register; in the version of the assembly language we are using, we can refer to this using the register-denotation %a6. The return address is stacked immediately 'below' this, i.e. in the adjacent four bytes of higher address. The actual parameters of the function call are found in succeeding higher-addressed locations, all of which may be referenced using a positive-valued offset from a6. For example, the instruction:

```
mov.l 8(%a6),%d0
```

will move the value of parameter 1 (obtained by applying the byte offset 8 to the address contained in register a6) into register d0. Conversely:

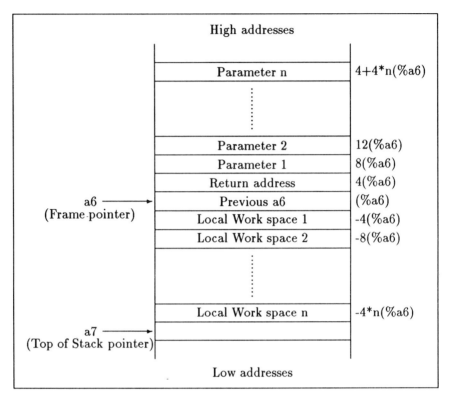

Figure 8.6   Stack space allocation after function call

```
mov.l %d1,-8(%a6)
```

will transfer a value from register d1 into location 2 of the local workspace
(obtained by applying the *negative* offset 8 to the frame base pointer).

To see how this might work in practice, consider first the simple C
program of Figure 8.7. The function ass(), in this example, has been
'commented out'; it is included for documentary purposes, to describe the
effects we expect of an assembly language routine that is called in its place.
ass() has three parameters: x and y are simple integer values, and z is a
pointer to a location whose contents are changed by the function.

When this function is called, the state of the stack is as illustrated
in Figure 8.8. The *actual* parameters b,c and &a (the address of a) are
stored at offsets 8, 12 and 16 from the frame base, corresponding to formal
parameters x,y and z. The first negative offset from the frame base is used
for the local variable, temp, declared within the function.

```
/* This program is going to be used to call an assembler
 * equivalent of the 'commented out' function 'ass'. */
#include <stdio.h>
extern void ass(int, int, int *);

main()
{
    int a,b,c;
    a = 1;
    b = 2;
    c = 3;
    ass(b,c,&a);
    printf("a = %d\n",a);
}

/*----------------------------------------------------------*/

/* An assembler equivalent of this routine is being used
 * void ass(int x, int y, int *z)
 * {
 *     int temp;
 *     temp = x+y;
 *     *z += temp;
 * }
 */
```

Figure 8.7   A C program to call an assembly-language routine

Figure 8.9 contains a listing of an assembly language version of the function `ass()`. Even to those unfamiliar with the 68000 assembly language we are using, the main features of this should be fairly clear. The first action of the routine is to use the `link` instruction to establish the new stack frame, allocating four bytes of local workspace (for the variable `temp`) and leaving the stack in the state illustrated in Figure 8.8. Thereafter, the actual parameters (`b`,`c` and `&a`), and this temporary working location, are referenced using appropriate offsets from the frame base register a6; d0 and a0 are the only other registers used, so no side-effects are inflicted on the calling program. Finally, the `unlk` instruction is used to return the stack to the state applying when the call was made, restoring a6 and a7 to their

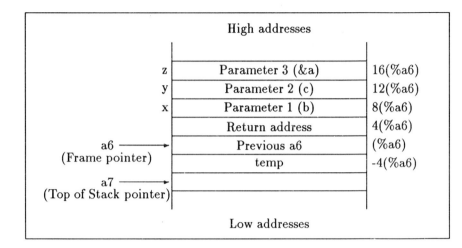

Figure 8.8   Parameters on the stack

previous values, and the **rts** instruction returns control to the C program.

Figure 8.10 provides a final example of a C program calling an assembly language routine. In this case, the routine **inc** has no parameters, but returns a result (in register d0). The routine also references a global variable, **counter**, declared in the C program; and the program illustrates the use of an assembler directive that provides the necessary information for the linker to fix this reference.

Again we must emphasize that all the details of these programs are implementation-dependent, including in particular the assembler notation and directives, and the register-use and store-allocation details of the C implementation. Good, locally available documentation should provide the equivalent information for the system you are using, but this is an area of programming in which particular care must be taken to avoid misunderstandings and consequent serious errors.

```
# This is a simple assembler routine which can be linked
# to a C program.

        global  _ass            # To know a symbol externally
                                # it must be declared with the
                                # global assembler directive.
                                # In C all user-declared global
                                # variables and functions are
                                # prefixed by an underscore
                                # character for the linker.
                                # Hence the assembler routine
                                # _ass will correspond to
                                # the C function ass.
_ass:
        link.l  %a6,&-4         # Allocate 4 bytes of local
                                # work space

        mov.l   8(%a6),%d0      # d0 = b;
        add.l   12(%a6),%d0     # d0 = b+c;
        mov.l   %d0,-4(%a6)     # temp = d0;

        mov.l   16(%a6),%a0     # a0 = &a
        mov.l   -4(%a6),%d0     # d0 = temp;
        add.l   %d0,(%a0)       # a = a+d0;

        unlk    %a6             # Deallocate local work space
        rts                     # Return
```

Figure 8.9   An assembly-language routine

```c
/* This program calls an assembler routine, illustrating
 * how an assembler program can access global variables. */

int counter = 0;

main()
{
  int i, last;
  for (i=0; i<100; i++) last=inc();
  printf("counter = %d\n",last);
}

/*------------------------------------------------------------*/

/* An assembler equivalent of this routine is being used
 *
 * int inc()
 * {
 *     counter++;
 *     return counter;
 * }                                                    */
```

```
# This simple assembler routine can be linked to the C
# program above.It illustrates how globals can be accessed.

         comm    _counter,4      # Use the assembler directive
                                 # comm to indicate a global
                                 # variable 'counter' of
                                 # size 4 bytes
         global  _inc            # To correspond to the C
                                 # function inc.
_inc:
         link.l  %a6,&0          # No local workspace needed
         addq.l  &1,_counter     # counter = counter+1;
         mov.l   _counter,%d0    # d0 = counter;
                                 # result is returned in d0
         unlk    %a6
         rts                     # Return
```

Figure 8.10   A C program with an assembly-language function

Index